Crystal Dill

Copyright © 2018 Crystal Dill

Printed in the United States of America

All rights reserved. No part of this publication may be reproduced, stored in a retrieval system, or transmitted in any form of by any means- for example, electronic, photocopy, recording- without the prior written permission of the Author. The only exception is brief quotations in printed reviews.

ISBN: 1717391494
ISBN-13: 978-1717391490

Unless otherwise noted, Scripture quotations are taken from The Holy Bible, New Living Translation, copyright © 1996. Used by permission of Tyndale House Publishers Inc. Wheaton, IL 60189. All rights reserved.

Scriptures marked NKJV is taken from the New King James Version. Copyright © 1979, 1980, 1982 by Thomas Nelson, Inc. Used by permission. All rights reserved.

Cover Design by Anna Friendt Art & Illustration

To my Heavenly Father, Jesus Christ and Holy Spirit.
Thank you for entrusting this work to me, leading me and training me.
It is Your Word that is a lamp unto my feet and I will follow You all the days of my life.
And to my wonderful husband, James and incredible son, Lincoln.
You both love and encourage me in the most beautiful ways.
Thank you.

CONTENTS

	Acknowledgments	i
1	Introduction	1
2	Vulnerability	7
3	Brokenness	15
4	Joy	24
5	Surrender	34
6	Repentance	48
7	Seek	61
8	Walk	82
9	Fulfill	95
10	Ignite	108
11	Echo	121
12	Who is Moses	133

Acknowledgments

Thank you daddy for doing my preliminary edits, encouraging me to clearly and concisely expound on my heart message. I admire your way with words and your intellect. It means so much to me that you were such a huge part of this journey. Anna, thank you for my cover design. You get me. You love Jesus. There's no one better. (ps. Check out the next page to learn more about Anna!) My other Anna for my back cover copy. You hit the mark with my heart message. Thank you.
Thank you to my Spiritual Mama's… you have helped challenge me, encourage me and prayed me up through this process!
Thank you for all of my family and friends who have helped cheer me on during this time. Your encouragement means the world and I truly appreciate each and every one of you.

About the Artist

Art has been and continues to be an integral and vital thread which has been interwoven into Anna's personal story and life journey. It has been a God-given gift that the Lord has used to give her hope from her past and has enabled her to share that same hope with others. God has used artwork in Anna's life to assist in the process of healing from a traumatic childhood marred by the sins of others as well as breaking free from suicidal depression, severe anxiety, alcohol abuse, and the commercial sex industry. She uses her artwork to shed truth and light on her healer, Jesus. To commission Anna and to view her work visit: *Anna Friendt Artwork and Illustration* (annafriendt.com).

Art is a gift to be shared which is why she has also founded a nonprofit organization called *Anchor 13 Studio* - a collaborative creative arts studio where Creatives create to partner with survivor-led nonprofit organizations that fight to abolish human sex trafficking as well as bringing hope, healing, and love to those who are in the commercial sex industry. Their mission: pointing the hearts of people towards the same kind of healing and restoration that Anna has been able to experience in her life, ultimately leading her to a life of victory and freedom. All proceeds from shopping the online shop at anchor13studio.com and purchasing artist creations go straight into financially supporting survivor-led organizations.

INTRODUCTION

The Burning Bush

  I found God in the dishes… well not really… I found God in college… *but*…. My burning bush moment was in a sink full of soapy dish water. However, instead of calling me out into the nations… He called me out… like exposed my wicked heart- called me out.

  You see, several months before I was elbow deep in bubbles and revelation, God had taken me from the career I thought I was destined for and very loudly and clearly said to my heart: "Crystal, you've lived <u>*your*</u> dream for a year, now it's time to live <u>*mine*</u>."

  So, I'm thinking, "Great!…. Ouch, Lord… but great!"
"So let's go! I'm ready! What will we do?!"

  Has God ever showed you something to come, or spoken something over you but then *seemed* to do the opposite?

  Well, to my heart, I heard Him say, "healing ministry"…

  My excited-self jumps right back in, 'Ok Lord! Let's go to the hospitals and pray for people, let's go out on the streets! I'm ready! People need to know your love! Let's go!" And…. *That's* when He called me home.

Home.

No car; which felt like no freedom for *this* social butterfly. A 3-year-old and a young marriage that had been a liiiiiittle bit neglected for a little too long.

It was in the dishes that I heard Him. It was in the dishes that I felt the bitterness in my heart like a rock that was stuck in my chest. The discontent. The nagging restlessness.

And then I heard His gentle voice whisper… "Why don't you worship me as you wash the dishes?" …

This is the part where He was calling me out. But He knows I needed His gentleness. He was basically saying, "Hey sweetheart… knock it off! Your attitude; you're all wrong. You don't like the way your marriage is going, you think things are unfair, you hate doing the dishes, you're tired, you're cranky, you're longing for something more… I know… just focus on me right now…"

And so I did… I grabbed my ear buds, turned on my favorite Pandora worship station and I washed those dishes. I washed them *so* good!

With each scrub of every plate, cup, or bowl; they became new again, just like the gunk that surrounded my heart began to dissolve. As I simply proclaimed the beauty of Jesus in my own heart and turned my focus and gaze to Him; the bitterness, the discontent, the anger, all washed away in the soapy water that day. And suddenly, love, peace, and joy began to rush back into my soul like a flood.

The icy cold heart I had been unknowingly wallowing in was melting away.

That was the beginning of a 5-year journey…a healing ministry to my weary heart. A journey at home; where God took the vulnerable broken pieces of my soul, softened my heart and taught me how to serve. He taught me what it was like to put my family as my number one ministry. They would always come first. They had to. They were the ones I interacted with the most. The ones who knew my ugly sides, and if I couldn't serve them, I couldn't serve anyone else well.

You see, at that time, I would have much preferred to go pray with the homeless man on the street corner than to pray for my husband- let alone try and work on our marriage that was gasping for air and longing for care. When it felt like God was stripping me of my dream… He was.

But what felt like a demotion was really a "graduation" into the next season of training ground. He knew I wouldn't listen. This is why He had to take it away from me like He did. It didn't feel good. It felt terrible; like the rug had been pulled from under my feet and I fell…. *Hard*! The kind of fall where your tailbone hits the wood floor and it takes your breath away for a good few seconds. A swift kick in my pants and a redirection.

> "When it felt like God was stripping me of my dream… He was."

Often though, God's promotion *appears* to be a demotion if we look at it through our natural, sometimes selfish lenses. However, living our lives for Jesus is contrary in that way. *"The first shall be last, and the last shall be first." (Matthew 20:16)* Things in God's realm are often the opposite of the world's ways of viewing things.

Look at the lives of David, Joseph, and Moses… David was looked down upon for being a young shepherd boy. Joseph was imprisoned wrongfully after being abandoned by his brothers and sold into slavery. Moses grew up in the palace, and chose exile for half of his life.

Yet, each of them, after a time of enduring the difficult

seasons, were rewarded greatly by God. David slew Goliath as a young boy, and grew to be the greatest King in Israel. Joseph became second in command in Egypt; Moses was instrumental in the deliverance of God's people out of Egypt.

After the humbling process, we learn to be content in *all* circumstances and keep our gazes fixed upon God. In my case, I had to learn to humbly serve God and my family. As we gain humility and keep moving forward with our gaze on Him, He allows us to step into the position He has prepared for us all along.

Once I graduated from the season of humbling and refining, I grew to absolutely **love** being at home. I am happy to say that I now find *joy* in doing the dishes! I love serving my husband and my son and I do my best to make our home a safe, cozy environment full of the love of God. It's my life ministry. Once I began to grow deeper with The Lord I began to see changes in the way I would respond to things and the desires of my heart shifted. I began to feel an atmosphere shift in my home. All of us did. My marriage began to strengthen and flourish. Love began to grow there. God's presence was changing our family. It's when we say, "Lord, I'm ready for heart surgery. Have your way!" that we begin to see change. God can truly move mountains when we start with *us*.

This journey of life at the core is truly about how we connect with God on a deeper level. A continuous graduation to a new level of intimacy with our Creator. He desires to be close to us, and He uses our circumstances to draw us to Himself through it all.

In this day and age, there is darkness all around us throughout the world. And as a follower of The Lord Jesus Christ, there is a hope and a light that can extinguish the darkness like nothing else can if only we would truly understand how to let that light shine.

I believe that there is a gross misconception and underestimation of what power lies in having a deep intimate relationship with The Living God. Through each chapter I'd like us to go on a journey of inner reflection where we look intently at ways that we can become more intimate with God. In what ways have we already established our relationship with God? How can we take it a step further? And finally, how could it affect the world around us if we never stop making this our aim and practice? Could we come together as believers with such unity on *this one thing* and see a breakthrough like never before?

    I believe we can. I believe that when we are laser focused on knowing God and loving Him with all that we are; we will find a peace that defies logic to all of the answers to our toughest questions and struggles.

The Mark of Moses...

Moses is an ordinary man who had an extraordinary relationship with The Living God.

We see as an example, from the time Moses was a baby that God had a plan for him. God does indeed have a plan for us as well; not just to use us to do mighty things and not to simply bless us, but He is a strategic God. He is a loving God who will go to great lengths to see His will in our lives be accomplished.

We too, just like Moses, can have an extraordinary relationship with The Living God. Because of His great love for us, we can know He will see His plan through and we will find that to God, we are not ordinary- we are created to be extraordinary! Yet this can only happen through our relationship with Him.

Let's take a look at the different ways God's love draws us into His presence through different points of our journey.

Vulnerability

"Vulnerability is a mark of intimacy with Me"

Vulnerability *is a mark of intimacy with our Maker. Where there is vulnerability there is a lack of pride. There is a letting go of ourselves, our own ideas and letting go of worry or fear of what others may think or what risks may be involved.*

To be vulnerable is typically defined as capable of being wounded as by a weapon, or difficult to defend.

Because of our self-protective human nature, we typically would never want to purposefully be vulnerable. We put emotional and mental barriers up to protect our ego, our heart, our pride, etc. We sometimes learn to be vulnerable with people whom we love because we find they do their best to protect us from being wounded. I'm sure we have conversely found ourselves in wounded positions when we've made ourselves vulnerable and open in certain human relationships. But even in the most trusting human relationships, we can find vulnerability uncomfortable.

However, vulnerability with God is entirely different. If we remove the negative connotation of being difficult to defend, and understand we don't want to defend ourselves *against* a loving God anyway, we want **Him** to defend us. Vulnerability is also defined in part as being easily affected by something; when we are easily affected by *God* we become clay in His masterful hands. The Latin word for vulnerable is **vulnerare** "to wound". Instead of being wounded *by* God we make ourselves easily affected by His loving heart to bring healing *to* our wounds that we experience from this world.

You know, in order to be vulnerable with God we need to *let go*. We need to stop worrying about what others think or how others are behaving and truly focus on Jesus. When The Lord started dealing with me in my marriage I had to let my walls down. I wanted to defend myself. I wanted Jesus to take *my* side- but He didn't. He simply beckoned me to come closer to Him. The more we lean in to Him and let go of our idols of comfort and control the freer we become.

When I first encountered this Living God, it was as if all of my walls came tumbling down and I became defenseless to His love and grace flooding into my life. I couldn't help but hear his gentle whispers to put away the junk clouding up my mind, heart and life; and respond to Him. He disarmed me of my self-preserving defense mechanisms and set me free, but it came with the cost of being vulnerable with Him. Letting Him prod and poke my wounded heart; to let Him do heart surgery on the deepest parts of me that I wouldn't let anyone see. He knew it all, He'd seen it all and I knew it. I could no longer pretend to be hidden, for He called me out.

> "...let Him do heart surgery on the deepest parts... no one sees."

In order to experience the true freedom He has for us we must lay down trying to defend ourselves, defend our sin, defend our 'rights' to ourselves, and allow the weapon of His Word to pierce through even to the bone and marrow (Hebrews 4:12). His Word is a sword, and when we are willing to be vulnerable with The Lord, the power of that Sword cuts through the junk we have allowed to grow, fester, manifest, and hide in the deepest parts of our heart, mind and soul.

Why would we welcome this vulnerability? When we finally understand the walls we have built up are truly harming us. When we come to the realization that the walls are *actually* protecting a growing spiritual cancer inside of us, instead of protecting ourselves; we will seek the only cure for it: His Sword.

When we make ourselves vulnerable *to GOD*, we allow Him room to work; dismantling our self-built walls of fear, pride, insecurity, inferiority, anxiety, doubt, etc.; that have kept us bound, often for as long as we can remember.

We tend to think that admitting our sins and depravity makes us weak or that it might be painful. Being vulnerable brings healing. And the healing process *does* reveal a level of pain; just as a wound that must be cleansed is excruciating. But this pain brings a more pure healing. We must allow this cleansing so no infection can take place in our spirits.

Truthfully, it is the most freeing step we can take with The Lord. It brings freedom in ways we had never imagined possible. Vulnerability with The Living God allows the cancer of selfishness and flesh to be cut out at the root. It is cut by The Word of God as we make Him our *actual* Lord. In full surrender asking Him to deal with the things that we simply cannot on our own. The Scripture says that when we confess our sins He is faithful and just to forgive us. (1 John 1:9)

Peter's first message after being empowered by The Holy Spirit was bold and full of conviction because he knew the power of being completely moldable in the hands of Jesus.

"So let everyone in Israel know for certain that God has made this Jesus, whom you crucified, to be both Lord and Messiah!' Peter's words pierced their hearts, and they said to him and to the other apostles, 'Brothers, what should we

do?'

Peter replied, 'Each of you must repent of your sins and turn to God, and being baptized in the name of Jesus Christ for the forgiveness of your sins. Then you will receive the gift of the Holy Spirit." Acts of the Apostles 2:36-38

Merely declaring Him as Savior is not enough. That does not indicate that we have much vulnerability with Him except admitting that we can sometimes do wrong and need to be saved from damnation. To make Him our *Lord* means that we are willing to be vulnerable to our core; in every area relinquishing the right to be captain of our own life.

In the beginning of Moses' journey he was extremely vulnerable with The Lord. He laid out *all* of his insecurities and ways he felt unqualified to the call that God had placed on his life. He didn't know what to say, He was worried what others would think, and he wasn't confident in his speaking ability; *anyone* else would have been better suited for this task. He divulged all of his own weaknesses, and admitted where he lacked. Yet, God revealed where the strength would come from. The Lord's response to the shortcomings of Moses was simply, "I AM". When our minds race with thoughts of insecurity, inferiority, worry, doubt, fear, God simply says, "But, I AM". I AM is the ultimate name of The God of the universe. There is no lack with Him. He is everything. He is able. He knows all of our thoughts and fears. When we don't think we are enough; *God is*. Moses had to fully let God take over, be completely vulnerable and allow The Lord to have full say in his walk and journey. Moses' strength would not come from his own abilities, it would come from The Lord, and that strength only grew throughout the journey as Moses developed intimacy with Him.

Once we take down our walls and let God reign in our spirit, our heart, and over our lives, we begin to have a new level of intimacy with The One Who created us. We activate a journey of trusting Him and experiencing Him like never before. It becomes a raw, real relationship with our Maker, instead of a religious duty or act.

God is the only One Whose opinion matters. When I think of godly vulnerability, and vulnerability with The Lord, I am reminded of David dancing in the streets without a care of what anyone thought. He was truly dancing for The Lord, being vulnerable with The Lord; not allowing insecurity to stop him from his beautiful form of worship. (2 Samuel 6:14)

So let's take some time to become vulnerable with The Lord. Let our walls down. Let Him in to do the work of cleansing and healing that we all need. Throughout the rest of this book, we will take a look at the life of Moses in different areas; I'll share some more personal stories of my journey, also in each chapter I offer prayer and a time of reflection with questions.

Prayer is not a fancy set of words to try to impress God. It is a being real with Him. Prayer is a muscle- the more we use it the stronger it becomes. It allows us to communicate directly with God and enter the supernatural, it is not mundane. It is our words and heart cries lifting up to the throne of Heaven, and when they are sincerely expressed from our hearts or from our mouths- God is moved.

King David prayed, *"Let my prayer be set before you as incense, the lifting up of my hands as the evening sacrifice." Psalm 141:2*

David is saying our prayers are something pleasing to God. He finds pleasure in our coming to Him in vulnerability.

"So let us come boldly to the throne of grace that we may obtain mercy and find grace to help in time of need." Hebrews 4:16

Jesus has granted us this access to come to The King. We should not take it for granted nor take it lightly. This is a great privilege that not even the Israelites had. Moses was their mediator then. But now Jesus gives us access to speak directly to God Himself.

He awaits us to take our vulnerability to the next level.

The Mark of Moses...

At the moment of the burning bush, Moses responds in complete awe, wonder and full surrender.

Moses made himself vulnerable and open to God's call, even though he didn't yet understand the gravity or depth of his journey. He was willing to be open to God's plan.

I think there are many things we allow to get in our way because we are worried of what people will think, or how they perceive us. Yet, God made you in His image. He knows your every imperfection, still loves you and will use you in spite of those things, often times He will use the weaknesses you have to His advantage.

Just like Moses, we are ordinary human beings. He exhibited the same fears and shortcomings that we can. Even after all of the miracles and wonders that The Lord eventually did through Moses; he is still a human. What makes him so extraordinary is the level of intimacy he developed through obedience with The Creator.

Let's Pray

Heavenly Father and Lord, tear down our secret walls, which we have built up knowingly or unknowingly around our lives. Help us to allow You access into our hearts at the deepest level. Let us be VULNERABLE with You, Lord! Strip away the works of the flesh in our lives. Remove pride, insecurity, inferiority, frustration, anger, lust, and any selfishness we try to hang on to that is only killing us, and quenching your Spirit inside of us.

Let Your Word and truth penetrate to the depths of our hearts so that we can truly walk in freedom, and experience a new level of intimacy with You. We surrender our rights to You as Lord, and ask that You would help us in areas we struggle. Encourage us and embolden us to become victorious in areas we have felt like failures. Help us to open up our hearts and become vulnerable to you, and prepare us to experience you like never before, in The Name of Jesus.

Reflect

In what ways have you been vulnerable with God?

Do you have Him at arm's length in any area of your life?

What areas are you trying to keep secret from Him?

In what ways or areas have you begun to be more vulnerable with Him?

Could you open up more and allow more healing or correction to happen? Do you have fears holding you back from this?

What steps will you take right now and throughout this week to increase your level of vulnerability with God?

What is God saying to you about vulnerability with Him?

Brokenness

"Brokenness is a mark of intimacy with Me"

*When we are **Broken**, we are more willing to be **Vulnerable** with God. In our brokenness, we open ourselves up to a deeper level of intimacy with our Creator. And as we do, He gains access to our heart - and our brokenness - so He can begin the deep healing work we need Him to do.*

To be vulnerable and find that we are broken can be a scary thought. Our culture tells us that we need to be strong, pick up our own broken pieces, glue ourselves back together, and march on. However, God has a different and more powerful plan.

Being broken isn't a sign of weakness either. It is a mark of intimacy with our Maker when we admit that we need *Him* in order to become whole again.

"The sacrifice you desire is a broken spirit. You will not reject a broken and repentant heart, O God." Psalm 51:17

In our brokenness, we can produce a godly sorrow. It is an amazing thing to have your heart so broken and tenderized that it breaks for what breaks God's heart. All the while God is moved with compassion for what hinders us. We see this displayed multiple times in the life of Jesus. He wept at the death of Lazarus, and became angry and full of emotion as the people were stricken with grief and mourning. He was moved with compassion toward those who needed healing from their diseases, whether physical, spiritual or emotional. He is a God of compassion! He cares about our brokenness.

Moses was so intimate with The Lord that he gained a special compassion for the things The Lord cares about. Remember when the Israelites demanded a golden calf? What was Moses' response? He defended The Lord. He ran down the mountain and in furious anger rebuked Aaron and the Israelites and broke the stone tablets The Lord had just written with His own finger. The Lord wasn't upset with Moses' reaction, because it was a just and holy anger. It was a friend defending a friend. I believe at that point, Moses' heart broke. Can you imagine the heartbreak of The Lord to see His people worship something they made on their own? Especially after He had just delivered them from their oppressors in Egypt. How quickly they turned away from Him and worshipped their own gods.

I believe we can *still* break God's heart to this day. When we put our work, our family, our friends, our worry, our comfort, our entertainment, even our *ministry* before God. When we put our one on one relationship with God on the back burner, I believe it hurts God's heart.

These things become heart idols when not given their proper place. We see in Revelation that King Jesus says, "I know your works… yet I hold this against you: You have left your first love." The NLT says it this way, "You don't love me or each other as you did at first!" He is talking to Christians who endured hardships without growing weary, who worked hard for His Kingdom, who even did not tolerate wickedness… yet He knew their hearts weren't passionate for Him.

In the story of Lazarus, Jesus heard of the death of his friend. Scripture says Jesus loved him; He was fond of him; they were friends. He was also friends with Mary and Martha. They spent time together; they had a relationship.

Yes, Jesus loved Lazarus, but he didn't rush back. He waited. The journey was long back to Judea. Lazarus was in the grave 4 days before Jesus met with Mary & Martha only to hear them say what my heart has also said: "If only you would've been here…"

I've been in a situation where I have had a conversation like this with God…

"Why didn't you answer my prayer?"
"Where were you?"
"If only you would've been there!"

I've doubted my faith to the deepest level. You see, I was asked to pray for a dying man. The Lord put it on my heart to pray for this man; a brother of a friend who then became my friend. He was diagnosed with a terminal disease. But there were a group of us full of faith; willing to stand with him and pray for healing. Believing for healing from a fatal disease takes a bold faith and seeing beyond circumstances. Hebrews 11:1 teaches us that faith is the evidence of things not seen. I had heard powerful testimonies from friends and other ministers of broken limbs growing back together and instantly healing, uneven legs stretching out and becoming even, blind eyes seeing, deaf ears opening, food multiplying, people being healed of deadly diseases and even people raising from the dead… I know He is a healing God! He is Jehovah Rophe. (Hebrew for The Lord God Who heals).

So with childlike faith I went to battle for this new friend. I prayed day and night, I visited him when he asked and eventually when he couldn't speak physically he would type through a machine and write to me via email. He would send me bold emails declaring his desire and faith for healing, but also with a heart that said, 'Lord, even if you don't I trust you because I know I'll be healed one way or the other.'

It was an intense time of prayer and growing deeper with The Lord. Trusting His voice in new ways. And even though it didn't end with my friend being healed on *this* side of eternity, I know he is dancing and declaring God's goodness in the presence of Jesus now.

The Lord called me to be by his side physically through prayer and friendship. The "end" is not what I anticipated but I know The Lord desired my obedience and for my ears to be fine-tuned to His voice. "This is the way, walk in it Crystal". (Isaiah 30:21) With that kind of faith I was able to love a man I hadn't previously known in a way he may have needed at the end of his life.

While the human person of Jesus was intimate friends with Lazarus, Mary, and Martha, He is our intimate friend in Spirit. So I think many of us can identify with what these women were feeling when we experience utter brokenness; the brokenness from unanswered prayers, or rather, prayers answered *differently* than we expected.

These people were broken and grieving. I think it is so important for us to feel and acknowledge all of the emotions that come along with our brokenness and ask God to help us grow from them as we receive healing from The Lord.

When there is a cry in our heart that seems to be unanswered, or answered in a different way or timeframe than we expected, we can feel betrayed, angry, frustrated, confused - even happy in the hope that is buried somewhere beneath the desperate sadness. There can be so many emotions that come forth out of brokenness and sometimes *all* of these emotions at once. It can be consuming if we do not have our hope secured in Christ. The verse that I cling to when I feel life can be too much to bear is: "…When my heart is overwhelmed, lead me to The Rock that is higher than I." (Psalm 61:2)

Instead of being overwhelmed, I remember how intimately I've come to know Jesus through the brokenness I've experienced. Because deep down, I know He would never betray me. I know He would never deceive me. I know He would only do things to prosper the ones He loves so very much; much more than I could ever imagine, or even have the capacity to love. So it is in the times of brokenness, we need to go back to steadfast trust in His sovereignty. We need to read what His Word says about Him and take Him at His Word.

We have all been broken at one time or another in this journey of life. I've been broken by my circumstances before. I've been completely broke financially. I've made mistakes in relationships. I've been actually homeless. Destitute, like Jesus. Although my experience was temporary, I was broken by uncertainty, rejection and judgment.

I've been broken by my own sin affecting others and hurting the ones I love with my own selfish choices. Seeing firsthand the repercussion for my disobedience had me broken, and I desperately needed the redemption that can only come from Christ.

I was certainly broken inside the moment I realized that Jesus Christ, the very Son of God allowed His body to be completely obliterated to the point of being unrecognizable. He took this on willingly because of my sin, yet also because of His deep love for me.

I was absolutely broken when I truly realized how Jesus allowed His blood to be poured out at Calvary, that He died of a broken heart because of the immense compassion He had for the burden of the world that rested on His human heart.

When I realized He desired me, my companionship, my soul, my heavenly citizenship, my talents, my gifts, my smile... Me - so much that He sacrificed *as* a man *for* me - I was broken.

One of my dearest friends shared an analogy of a Japanese art called Kintsugi. It is when a precious piece of china, for instance, a teacup, is shattered or broken into pieces. Instead of disposing of it, they create a special gold paste and carefully reconstruct the teacup and piece it back together. Once cured, the brokenness of the teacup is highlighted, creating a beautiful, unique design. The teacup is once again useful to drink out of, and completely unique in its newly designed restoration.

Just as the fallen state of the world we live in can bring us to brokenness, our Creator, being the Designer that He is, takes our broken pieces and fits them back together to create something unique, beautiful, and useful once again. He does not dispose of us in our brokenness. He does not ignore our brokenness. He does not try to hide our brokenness. He restores us, more useful than ever, even more beautiful than ever, highlighting the fact that we cannot be useful apart from His design. Showing all those who gaze upon His restorative work, that they too can be made whole if they give their shattered pieces to The One Who has a divine design for their lives too.

> "He does not dispose of us in our brokenness."

Counterfeit glue can wear out over time, if we try to put our own pieces back together. We might miss a small fragment here or there. We are faulty, we are human. When we can be vulnerable enough to admit that we are faulty, and admit that we are broken, we then turn over the broken pieces to The One Who created us in the first place. Who knows better than *He* to piece us back together? And since it was originally His design, He can rebuild us even stronger than before. He knows us better than we know ourselves!

I will praise You, for I am fearfully and wonderfully made!
Psalm 139:14

The Mark of Moses...

Through Moses' extensive list of shortcomings, The Lord reminds him that He is <u>not</u> making a mistake by assigning this very dangerous top secret mission of deliverance to him.

The Lord reminds Moses that He is with Him, that He is Who He says He is, and He patiently gives Moses signs to assure him that He is truly being called to this great task.

Let's Pray

Lord, help us in our brokenness. Your word says that you heal the brokenhearted and bind up their wounds. (Psalm147:3 NKJV) Allow us not to hide in shame from the brokenness we experience. Help our hearts and minds to process through the emotions that can come with being broken or humiliated. Allow our pride to melt away, and become vulnerable to You, The Only One Who can make us whole again. Begin your restorative work in our hearts; we give you every shattered piece, as painful as it can be. Even if we do not sense clarity at the current moment, we cling to Who You are. Forgive us for any accusations we have placed upon You. Forgive us for not trusting you at any point in our journey of brokenness.

Help us to cling to Your Word. We are *more* than conquerors (Romans 8:37). You are not a man that you can lie (Numbers 23:19).

You love us. You work ALL things together for our good (Romans 8:28). You are the Author and Finisher of our faith (Hebrews 12:12). We were created for good works in Christ Jesus (Ephesians 2:10). We cling to these truths found in your Word. Be our Comforter, Be our help in time of need. I pray we would open up our hearts to You, for You are the only One who can mend our broken hearts. As we allow ourselves to be vulnerable to You, continue to show us that we can trust You with our broken pieces. We trust in You with ALL of our hearts, and do not lean on our own understanding, but in all our ways we acknowledge You, and trust that You will direct our paths. (Proverbs 3:5)

Thank you Lord! In Jesus' name we pray… amen

Reflect

How have you been broken in your life?

When you've been broken, how have you turned to God and given Him your broken pieces?

If you have yet to give Him some broken pieces of your heart, why do you feel you've held back?

Have you blamed God or yourself for any brokenness you've experienced?

In your own words, write down the broken areas where you would like God to give you the healing you are in need of. (emotionally, mentally, physically, spiritually)

   Have you forgiven others or yourself for the broken experiences in your life?

JOY

"Joy is a mark of intimacy with Me"

*The fruit of **Joy** is a mark of intimacy with The Lord. We can find joy in the midst of difficulty. We can develop strength through brokenness. The Scripture says that the joy of The Lord <u>IS</u> our strength (Nehemiah 8:10) and that His strength is made perfect in our weakness or brokenness (2 Corinthians 12:9). In other words, joy is the strength we need to overcome our **Brokenness.***

I have seen joy manifest through a child's unrestrained laughter. I have also seen joy manifest through the inner strength of a spiritual warrior losing a dearly loved one. I had never seen this dimension of joy before, until one of my dearest friends lost her father. He meant the world to her. And although cancer took his life suddenly, the events that led up to his death were nothing short of miraculous, and God was glorified in a way I have never seen before. The joy in the midst of sorrow that was displayed through their sure hope and absolute knowing of where her daddy was going was a beautiful display. The strength I saw in and through her was pure joy. She was grieving but hopeful, steadfast in prayer, soaking up every moment with him she could, and constantly listening for her Heavenly Father's voice and direction.

James tells us to *"consider it pure joy, my brothers and sisters, whenever you face trials of many kinds, because you know that the testing of your faith produces perseverance. Let perseverance finish its work so that you may be mature and complete not lacking anything." (James 1:2-4)*

The trials we inevitably face give us a choice. Will we choose to wallow in misery and feel defeated? Or will we choose to embrace the joy that The Lord provides for us, knowing that there will be a wonderful maturing as we persevere? When we choose to see with spiritual eyes and with an eternal perspective, we are blessed as we become more able to endure, persevere and mature through trials.

In John 16:24 Jesus says, *"Ask and you shall receive, that your joy may be full."* When we keep an open connection with Jesus through the Holy Spirit we come into alignment with *His desires*. When we do this, we can then have confidence to ask Him, and we know that His promises say to ask and we shall receive. The key here is being so close with Him that we understand His heart and His desires.

In John 15, Jesus talks about abiding in the vine; which is Himself. He says if we abide in Him we will bear abundant fruit; apart from Him we can produce nothing, we can do nothing, and we will become nothing. It will all be burned up if we attempt to be fruitful apart from abiding in Him.

However, *if we abide in Him, and His words abide in us*, we will ask for anything, and it will be done. He says if we keep His commandments we will abide in His love, just like He kept His Father's commandments, and abode in His Father's love. He then says, "These things I have spoken to you, *that your joy might remain* in you, and that *your joy might be FULL.*" So *again* we see Jesus teaching that when we are close and intimate with The Lord, like fruit from the vine, we receive true joy. The fullness of joy.

I recently heard someone say joy is like a bulletproof vest; we can go through seemingly unbearable circumstances and yet remain in joy when we are connected to Jesus. We can still bear the fruit of joy because of our eternal hope. Not only our eternal hope in our destination, but because we know Who has the victory, and we receive the Word that says we are more than conquerors through Him Who loved us (Romans 8:37). Joy is not a feeling, it is not happiness. Happiness can manifest as a *byproduct* of joy, but joy is not as fleeting as the feeling of happiness. Joy is a fruit of the Spirit. (Galatians 5:22) And as Jesus said, God is glorified when we bear much fruit, and we bear fruit by abiding in the vine.

Joy is a choice and a fruit of the Spirit to bear. But we must choose to *abide* in order to receive it. Because our circumstances can vary, our joy must remain steady.

We can find joy knowing that Jesus hears our prayers, and that when we *abide* in Him we can experience abundant fruit regardless of our circumstances.

But therein-lies the secret. To experience this joy, abiding in Him is key.

In order to bear that spiritual fruit, we must abide in the Vine, and have a close intimate relationship with Him. When we think of a grape vine, the grapes connected directly to the vine are firm, juicy, and healthy. The grapes that fall to the ground become bruised and begin to shrivel. Staying deeply connected to Jesus is key for a healthy spiritual life.

> *"But therein-lies the secret. To experience this joy, abiding in Him is key."*

A plant cannot disconnect from its roots and survive. A flower plucked from the garden will only last for a short time before it withers away. We, like the flowers of the earth, cannot survive as a beautiful flower for very long apart from the roots of our Father; but once we have been firmly planted in The Lord, rooted down, we grow, we bloom, and we flourish and produce beautiful foliage and fruit.

When we take inventory of the current fruit we are producing, or lack thereof, how do we cultivate more fruit? If fruit is something we are supposed to bear, then why do we so often falter, fail, and struggle?
The answer?

Our sin is smothering out the Spirit of God in our mortal bodies. Plain and simple.

In 1 John it says *"all unrighteousness is sin" (1 John 5:17)*. Disobedience is sin: in 1 Samuel 15:23 we see that rebellion or disobedience is considered as sinful as witchcraft. Samuel is having a conversation with King Saul who was obeying *part* of what God commanded but *not entirely*.

Isn't it easy to do this nowadays? We cherry-pick the Word of God so it fits our life, find what makes *sense to obey and disregard the rest*. But if we desire true joy, there is something special about obeying and abiding in The Lord.

Samuel says to Saul's justification, "What is more pleasing to The Lord: your burnt offerings and sacrifices or your obedience to His voice? Listen! Obedience is better than sacrifice, and submission is better than offering..." (1 Samuel 15:22).

In other words, your service to God isn't as important as your heart condition. And one big reason is because Christ came to bring us fullness of joy! He wants us to experience His abundant life full of the fruits of the spirit! He doesn't want us under condemnation of the law and to obey out of obligation. Jesus said if you *love* me you will obey me, because He knows that there is a deep joy when we walk closely with Him. And out of that love and obedience flows joy. When you love someone deeply, you choose to live in a way that honors them and makes them smile, it brings you *both* joy. This is how He desires our hearts to be toward Him.

So we must return to our first love, check ourselves, and say *"Oh Lord, search my heart and see if there be any wicked way in me." (Psalm 139:23)* Then we must come back and choose to abide in the Vine.

It is a *choice* to obey, not a natural inclination. Jesus wouldn't have commanded for us to abide in the vine, if it were not a *decision* we could make. A command is something used to help us fight against the sinful nature. It is not something we do instinctively. And He was speaking to the disciples not to unbelievers. If we are true disciples of Jesus, we must continuously put effort in to abiding in Him. That is the only way to bear much fruit; to be in a *constant* and growing relationship with The Vine.

In 2 Corinthians, Paul talks about how he is rejoicing that his letter of rebuke led the Corinthians to repentance through godly sorrow. He wasn't happy that they had to be broken, but that their brokenness led them to repent.

Oftentimes our situations and circumstances that lead us to brokenness also lead us to repentance, and through repentance comes the greatest joy of all! We find freedom when we repent of the things that have caused us to be broken, and when we've been broken by the world we find freedom by finding our strength in The Lord.

A little bit later in the same letter to the Corinthians, Paul talks about the church in Macedonia, sharing how they were being tested by many troubles: being very poor, **but**, filled with _abundant joy,_ which then overflowed in the form of rich generosity.

Moses was connected to The Lord throughout much of his life, and almost the entire journey with God was face to face intimacy. He exhibited joy when he asked The Lord to reveal His glory. What a beautiful moment of intimacy where we see the authenticity of craving The Lord's presence over anything. He was completely caught in the moment of being face to face with The Lord.

He knew the secret of staying connected to The Vine. He knew his strength would be found in the joy of The Lord's presence. He faced his brokenness and vulnerability; and through staying connected to The Lord he gained much strength.

Moses was open with The Lord, displayed his insecurities, and God overcame it all. His insecurities were replaced with a steadfast joy which produced strength enough to lead the Israelites out of slavery and into the Promised Land.

"In your presence is fullness of joy." Psalm 16:11

Joy is produced when we stay connected to The Lord. It is a fruit that is actually one of the more vital ones for a healthy relationship with Jesus, which I believe oftentimes, gets overlooked. Because Joy is often mistaken for a feeling of happiness, I believe we think we can do without it, or if we are experiencing happiness, we think we've got it. Or maybe we consider it less essential because we equate it with feelings or emotions.

There was a period of time where my family and I were displaced. I guess technically you could say we were 'homeless'. During that time we experienced rejection, dejection, a roller coaster of emotions. One minute I was confident in the fact that God had a plan, the next minute I was wondering what was taking Him so long. We were looked down upon, ridiculed, and misunderstood. It was a difficult time. However, the moments where I gave in to the negative emotions were fleeting. I knew *that I knew* God is good and that He was leading us. In fact, there were many incredible supernatural events leading us through that season. There were plenty of closed doors, but then at just the right time, the right door would open and God's grace would flood in and sustain us through the next few days. It ended up being exactly 2 months to the day that we went from being uprooted and displaced to being transplanted into a new place of promise. Throughout that entire journey I had people watching us go through that and day in and day out they asked me, "how do you keep it all together?" … "How are you so calm?" … "How are you still smiling?"… My answer?

Joy.

"Always be full of joy in the Lord. I say it again- rejoice! … Don't worry about anything; instead, pray about everything. Tell God what you need, and thank him for all he has done. Then you will experience God's peace which exceeds anything we can understand. His peace will guard your hearts and minds as you live in Christ Jesus. And now, dear brothers and sisters, one final thing. Fix your thoughts on what is true, and honorable, and right and pure, and lovely, and admirable. Think about things that are excellent and worthy of praise… I know how to live on almost nothing or with everything. I have learned the secret of living in every situation whether it is with a full stomach or empty, with plenty or little. For I can do everything through Christ who gives me strength." Philippians 4:4-8, 12-13

Paul says to be content in *all* circumstances which teaches us that we cannot allow our circumstances to dictate how we relate to God. James 1:2 says to consider all of our trials as joy, and as we grow in Christ and see the fruit of persevering through our trials; that is when we can really understand why we consider them as joy. As strong believers in Christ we can still obtain joy in the midst of heartache and turmoil. Joy is staring directly into the eye of the storm without wavering. Joy is a steadfast warrior determination against all odds. Joy is a sure knowing of the identity you have as a child of God. Joy is knowing your outcome is victorious regardless of what it looks like in the natural, because in the supernatural you are a child of The King, and therefore, no weapon that is formed against you will prosper *(Isaiah 54:17)*.

Joy is having your face set like a flint, even when the enemy is shouting taunts and threats at you.

*Joy **is** strength.*

Because when the believer looks into the storm, they see The Redeemer creating order out of chaos. They see, even though the enemy may surround them, The Lord has the enemy surrounded in an even greater number. Their eye isn't fixed *on* the storm - it is fixed on *the One Who is sure to calm the storm*.

Joy is laughing in the face of the things meant to destroy you because you know The God you serve has *taken* the keys of death and hell. (Revelation 1:18) He has given you the promise to step on the neck of the devil. (Romans 16:20) Joy is the absolute awe and anticipation of seeing your Victorious King Jesus on His white horse, illuminating in triumphant glory, and knowing this Warrior King *loves you* and you know Him intimately. He is yours, and you are His. Nothing compares to Him, and there is a pure unrivaled joy in knowing Him personally.

The Mark of Moses

It was when Moses was feeling the weakest that God would remind him who *He* is as The Lord…what joy we find when we allow God to be our strength.

In Exodus 6:3, The Lord tells Moses, "I appeared to Abraham, Isaac and Jacob as El-Shaddai (God Almighty), but I did not reveal my name, YAHWEH, to them.

This is a level of intimacy that can easily be glossed over. Throughout their journey in the wilderness, The Lord revealed many aspects of Himself to Moses as Peace, Provider, Banner etc… What a great privilege to know The Lord in the layers of depth that He reveals to us. What a joy to truly know The Lord!

Let's Pray

Dear Father in Heaven, as David prayed, restore unto us the JOY of our salvation! The Psalms say to enter into your gates with thanksgiving and into your courts with praise! So I thank you Lord for all you have done for us. Let us not ever forget the blessings you have graciously given to us! Let us see Your mighty hand when it has moved in our lives, and when it continues to. Lord thank you for being strong in our weakness. Thank you for giving us strength and mounting us up on wings like eagles as we wait upon You, Oh Lord. Praise you for WHO you are! Praise you Jehovah Shalom! You are our peace that surpasses understanding. Praise you Jehovah Jireh, Lord, You Provide! Praise you Jehovah Rohpe! Lord you heal us! Praise you Jehovah Nissi! For, You are our banner! We lift you up high, we lift your name up, and we praise You because you deserve all the honor, the glory, and the praise.

Lord teach us to find strength through the fruit of joy. Jesus, show us how to find joy in the midst of sorrow, and through clinging to the joy of the greater picture, strengthen us.

Thank you Lord for eternal hope - not a narrowed perspective eternal life, which is much more than just a resting place after we pass from this life to the next, but Lord, eternal hope of the *supernatural life*. The supernatural life is here and now, *and* forevermore - and we are your children so we have this hope - we have this joy! Thank you Lord for this joy. I pray right now for anyone reading this, that they would experience supernatural joy like they never have before, if they are currently broken, or in a desert season, Lord would you bring them a refreshing of the well of your Spirit that would quench even the driest of hearts. Thank you in advance for the outbreak of joy, manifesting in strength, in laughter, in sure hope, in faith, in the supernatural, in the Name of Jesus…. Amen.

Reflect

Let's take inventory of current fruit in your life
Are you currently experiencing: love, joy, peace, patience, kindness, meekness, goodness, faithfulness, gentleness, self-control (as found in Galatians 5)?

If any of the previous spiritual fruits are lacking, write them here and why they might be lacking.

Which do you feel are the strongest or most abundant fruits in your life?

Going back to the scripture referenced before, is there any unrepented sin in your life that may be hindering the fullness of fruit in your life?

Specifically in relation to joy, how have you experienced joy through a painful circumstance?

How do you think you could find joy in the brokenness in your life?

If you find this difficult, what perspective shift could you make to help you receive the encouragement from James to 'consider all our trials as joy?

Surrender

"Surrender is a mark of intimacy with Me"

*It is my **Joy** to lay my life down. To lay down my life, is to say "Lord, I want <u>Your</u> will, not my own." For it is not I who lives, but Christ who lives in me. (Galatians 2:20) To Surrender what I think is best, for what God actually knows is best. For His ways are higher than my ways, and His thoughts are higher than my thoughts (Isaiah 55:8-9). This is full and total **Surrender**.*

      Moses laid his entire life down to follow the call of Yahweh. He left his family and shepherding life and accepted God's mission. Once he heard the call in the burning bush, he couldn't turn back. Even though he gave God all of his excuses, he chose to trust The Lord and live a surrendered life to help God's mission in freeing His people.

      In 1 Peter 4:13 we are encouraged to **rejoice** that we partner with Christ in His suffering, so that we will have the wonderful *joy* of seeing His glory when it is revealed to the entire world. This *partnering is a surrender* to the life that He has died to give us; the surrendered life to Christ.

      John the Baptist's life was laid down for The Lord. His purpose was to pave the way for The Messiah. In the third chapter of John we hear him express that he is not the messiah, but that he is like the best man at the wedding, who is able to hear the vows exchanged between the bride and the bridegroom, and he says,

"Therefore this joy of mine is fulfilled. He must increase, but I must decrease." John remains a humble servant of The Lord, and expresses it is his joy to do so. (John 3:29-30)

Likewise, when Paul was writing to the Philippians he says, "Yes, if I am being poured out as a drink offering on the sacrifice and service of your faith, I am glad and *rejoice* with you all." (Philippians 2:17). Paul laid his life down for the cause of Christ to fill the hearts of His people, and he rejoiced in the sacrifice and surrender to The Lord.

We see in Hebrews 12:2 the joy of Jesus Himself, "…looking unto Jesus, the author and finisher of our faith, **who *for the joy* that was set before Him endured the cross**…"

Throughout his journey Moses was asked to do numerous things for The Lord and time and time again the scripture says, "And Moses did just as The Lord commanded him." His walk with God was a beautiful picture of total surrender.

Through my journey with God I have had many, many, many… points of surrender. And each time I choose to surrender another aspect of my life to God, I become a little closer to Him. As we continue to surrender and get to know Him deeper, we get to know a new aspect of Who He Is. Surrender is exciting! God can never be totally figured out. He is unfathomable. He is incomprehensible. He isn't one dimensional; He is far too great for that. I'm thankful for the journey I get to partake in that allows me to get to know Him continuously.

There is one point in my journey that was possibly one of the most significant in regards to the path that I am on. I do not believe I would've started my company, Double Take, nor that I would even be writing this book now, had God not intervened and urged me to surrender to His plan. It was several years ago that I had achieved a longtime dream of mine. I was in the top 2% of the company that I was a part of, and had achieved a higher up leadership status. I had finally achieved it! I was just getting my career started, I was going to make great money, be happy doing what I loved, and mostly work from home! I was going to achieve more dreams, prizes, and freedom than I had ever thought possible! I was going to also help other people do the same, and be able to share all about my faith on the journey! I even touted proudly how I kept my values as God first, family second and career third. I prayed hard, I worked hard, and I knew since this was such a great thing, there is *no way* God could oppose it!

And yet, exactly one year after I had achieved the status of leadership, achieved ***my*** dream… everything began to crumble. It didn't seem to be a steady decline into failure; but a supernatural ***dead stop***.

I remember going to a Wednesday night prayer meeting at our church, and begging God to do a miracle to keep my company status, to keep my dream alive. I went up for prayer and was hoping she would team up with me and pray for a miracle for God to make this dream continue… however, God had given me a truly wise person to pray over me that night. This young woman prayed, "Lord, let Your will be done…"

It sounds funny now- but I didn't like that prayer. Suddenly I became aware of the deep down realization that this might *not* be God's best for me. But I couldn't see past my own desires in that moment. I could not reconcile at that time that God wouldn't let me have the desires of *my* heart!

God had taken me through a process of inner searching through that time. He had even led one of my best friends and sisters in Christ to visit my last business meeting and do a fun coaching exercise with us. This exercise consisted of us being asked a series of questions, and writing down responses. At the end you could clearly see a pattern of responses and were able to categorize your top 3 values.

Guess what mine were? Career first… Family second… God third… Completely opposite of what I had always proudly proclaimed I had done!

If I'm honest with myself, when I look back, my values were off in my heart more than anything. I feel like truly it was career, throw my family on the back burner and hope they don't notice, and cram God in my 'doing my church attending duties.' My relationship with God had actually become *religious* without my knowing. What I mean by religious is that it was just a routine, something that I did out of habit, or to make myself *feel* better. Truly, when I look back at my faith at that point, I feel like it was as 2 Timothy 3:5 says:

"… having a form of godliness but denying its power…"

I had a severe reality check at that point, and began to search my heart. ***How*** have I allowed this to happen? How could God possibly be *last* on my list right now? This couldn't be true.

However, through His gentle Spirit, He showed me that indeed I was not perfect. *(Imagine that!)* Truly, the way I had been doing things, was wrong and self-focused instead of God-focused.

And He spoke something so clearly to me. I will never forget it as long as I live. He told me, "Crystal… You have been living *your* dream for 1 year… now it's time that you live *Mine*!"

I could not argue with what I so clearly heard in my spirit. It was at that point that I began my journey of true surrender.

And it was about 3 years of a humbling and refining process, where God kept me at home. He used the time of me being at home to teach me how to truly put God at the center of my life, and keep my family the number 1 ministry over everything that I would ever do; including ministering to others.

Sometimes as followers of Jesus, I think that we see someone hurting and think that they need us, when in all actuality; the most important mission is right in front of us at home. Sometimes we don't want to admit it or face it because at home there are troubles, arguments, annoyances, disrespect etc. But that is the point! What are we doing about it?! We must take authority over the spiritual atmosphere of our homes and families! We are children of God! We must know Him and be confident in our position in Christ.

Ministering to Susie down the street going through the loss of a loved one, or Kim who is going through a breaking marriage isn't going to fix *my* household! But that was my problem, and I'm willing to bet there are others a lot like me.

You may feel overwhelmed with the problems under your own roof, but feel good when you can encourage someone experiencing a hard time. While I'm not saying it's impossible to help another brother or sister in need while still dealing with troubles in your own family- the point is *it needs to be dealt with!* And The Lord faithfully showed me that it needed to be dealt with *first*, over other ministry opportunities. There is a war going on in the homes of God's people and we need to be vigilant in *not* allowing the enemy to have any footing there.

My heart was and still is *so* for loving people. So I was so excited to be there for others, help them, listen to them, pray for them, and be a vessel for God to minister to their hearts. However, all the while, my family was actually beginning to suffer. My marriage was being neglected in some ways, which was making my whole family hurt. Truly, God had to humble me to show me that if I would actually, *"Seek first the Kingdom of God and its righteousness that all these things would be added to me." (Matthew 6:33)*

He had for me, a healthy and successful marriage, a happy husband and son, a thriving spiritual life, a flourishing business, and ministry. But He had to reveal all of the disgusting areas of my heart that I was holding back before He could allow me access these blessings.

I was too busy focusing on how difficult everyone else was being around me, than focusing on my own problems. My heart was truly hard and I didn't even know it. I would've rather been out in the world helping people who I felt wanted it, or even deserved it. Don't we get indignant like that sometimes? Thinking we can help people when they *earn it*. We can be sweet and servant hearted when they show me they really will appreciate my efforts. That is where I was, and truly friends- that is a *selfish* kind of love, not the *Jesus* kind of love.

There was pride there, there was rebellion there, and if you knew me personally, you probably wouldn't have detected it. But, my husband sure could! *(Aren't spouses great at detecting each other's weaknesses?)*

Of course, in the beginning of this process, anything he tried to point out in me I only saw in him, I could not *possibly* have these ugly traits. But thanks be to God that He is patient with us, and if we really want *His* will, and we ask Him for it, and do the work to surrender, He is faithful to reveal the ugly things in our hearts so we can repent. There is a response required as God opens our hearts. It must be a partnership.

The Lord began to take me deeper with Him. As He would show me the areas where my heart was hardened or wrong, I would repent, and ask for His help. The example of doing the dishes in the beginning of the book sums this up. I will never forget it; it was a significant lesson in intimacy with Jesus and keeping my family my first ministry.

I began to enjoy doing things *"as unto The Lord" (Colossians 3:23)*, and serving my family through worshipping God by caring for our home. It was no longer a burden to me, but a calling.

Since then, my heart has not changed. I still love caring for our home, which is caring for my family. I am not perfect, but I will never forget if I start to slip, that I must remember to keep God at the center, and keep my family as my first ministry. They are the most important gift God has ever called me to steward over.

A few years after my training season, God finally placed a new dream deeply within my heart: Double Take. He showed me how I can use my gifts and talents as a makeup artist for His glory. At first, I was confused with how makeup could in any way actually be used for ministry. But I was simply obedient and began to make a business out of makeup artistry. When I sat down with a good friend of mine who beautifully branded the company God had prompted me to start, she helped me visualize what Double Take could *really* be!

I realized that I found joy in applying makeup to women because I am passionate about enhancing the natural beauty of women. The reaction of my clients is what captivated my heart. Some would look into a mirror and gasp. Others would have tears begin to well in their eyes. Others would say they had not felt this beautiful since their wedding day- some not even this beautiful *on* their wedding day. I loved watching them discover that they truly were beautiful. Makeup isn't what made them beautiful. It is how they were created by God- for beauty. They *are* beautiful. But once they caught a glimpse of this understanding- their inner beauty began to cause a glow that worked its way to the outside.

It was then that I realized it was going to be much more than makeup artistry. I knew my heart was to minister to women and others about who they are in Christ, and I knew I loved to write. I felt in my heart there would be more, and not surprisingly, but amazingly enough, about a year after I had been obedient and started the company, I was asked to speak at a small women's conference. I knew God was developing something big, and I am only watching God mold it year after year.

What an exciting life we can live when we truly surrender! And the excitement isn't found in how well we are known or the projects we get to be a part of. Our worth and adventure isn't found in our social status, how many likes we have on Facebook or how many followers we have on Instagram. Our worth, our adventure, our identity: it is all found in Him!

When we truly surrender, and allow Him to work in our hearts, God can take us to heights never imagined, and dreams only He can dream up for us! Do I think that ***my*** dream was a mistake? Absolutely ***not***! Because I pursued my dream the way that I did, I gained skills and acquaintances that I believe are vital for the role of Double Take. Nothing is wasted with God and a surrendered heart. He will use it all!

Had I not had to go through the process of letting go of what I thought was best for me, I wouldn't have received the freedom of dreaming even bigger than I had ever imagined and experiencing new dimensions of intimacy with God. I also would not have been humbled, molded and shaped in the way that I was by Him.

How often do we miss something greater? A greater peace. A greater love for our current situation. A greater acceptance of where we are. A greater enjoyment of the life God has for us. If we would simply surrender to Him- we would truly embrace where we are on our journey. Paul said that he learned to be content no matter what his circumstances came to be.

I am wondering though, in our culture of instant gratification and doing "what makes *me* feel alive" and "what makes *me* happy"; if people are experiencing *true* surrender.

Surrender is truly, sanctification. I don't hear that word very often anymore because it can be difficult to grasp. It takes sacrifice; it's usually painful and uncomfortable. Sanctification is setting something apart, to become holy. In this case, I'm talking about setting ourselves apart, to allow God to make us holy.

Surrender and sanctification go hand in hand. As we surrender to The Lord, we are continuously submitting to His will, and therefore, setting ourselves apart for His work. It is a sacrifice. A sacrifice of our will, our pride, our flesh.

It hurts! It is not fun nor is it easy to lay aside our desires or realize where we need God to prune us and help make us better. But it is *so* necessary. The pain of purification is worth the end result! We become smoother, lovelier, wiser, kinder, gentler, and stronger.

The question becomes, are we truly willing to *sacrifice* for God? When Jesus sacrificed *it all* for us, how can we not?

Most of us are willing to sanctify our Sunday's… some of us sanctify *parts* of our lives… "Oh, but Jesus… don't take away **this** pleasure!" We can't imagine He may want us to surrender something that seems good to us, or maybe it seems harmless. But if we will truly surrender, we will ask the *scary* questions. What about *this*, Jesus? Is this ok in my life?

Some of us sanctify the public part of us, but once we are alone, our true character reveals no change has been made by the power of The Holy Spirit. And sadly enough, some of us don't even give Him Sunday… we think: "I already *gave* Him my belief… I said the prayer… *why* should I give Him any more? What *more* could He possibly want from me? How could He possibly require more of me? He knows what I give my family, my career, my friends; I give to the local charity… How could He ask me of *more*?! I didn't sign up for this…"

> "The question becomes, are we truly willing to sacrifice for God?"

I've been in this place, you guys. It's easy to sit in this place. But I'm asking these prodding questions to provoke you to pray and seek Him in a deeper way.

You did believe on Him… you did call out to Him at one point… but why did you?

The day you first called out to Jesus, *something* pricked your heart, *something* moved in you; and truthfully, at that point your soul awakened and the foundations of your soul trembled at the realization of your need for The Creator of your soul to rescue you.

When we first hear the voice of Jesus, it feels something like the trembling of our soul shook the crumbling rocks away from the tender heart that was once formed *by* God, *for* God. Then our spirit began to cry out, "LORD! Creator! It's *YOU* I've needed all this time! I'm made for *more* than just living for the weekend, I'm made for *more* than just working to retire, and I'm made for more than just the daily grind of life. I'm made for more than only serving those I *choose* to, I'm made for more than only serving myself…"

And God says, "*YES!* Take up your cross and follow me… if you *lose* your life for my sake you will find it!"

But we look back… We ponder upon our past and sometimes can think it would be better to go back to that. The Israelites did this. After their delivery from Egypt they grew tired and weary and longed to go back to having all of their former pleasures, even if it meant going back to their slavery. Why do we look back in the same way? Because when the invitation came, we only gave the *hurting* part of our heart, we didn't let Him expose the whole thing…

In the book: Driven By Eternity, by John Bevere, he discusses the reality of the 'incomplete gospel' of today.

"It's not only those who've never heard or refuse to believe the gospel who are in bondage. Many typical 'converts' of this generation are enslaved to sin as well. We've created this dilemma by neglecting to proclaim the full message of what it truly means to follow Jesus. Many assume they are free when in reality they aren't, and the evidence is in their lifestyles. Jesus says:

"I assure you, most solemnly I tell you, whoever commits and practices sin is the slave of sin. Now a slave does not remain in a household forever.…So if the Son liberates you then you are really and unquestionably free." (John 8:34-36)
If someone habitually sins, that is evidence he is still a slave to sin. He is not a son, for his true nature hasn't changed. He may think he is free because he confessed a sinner's prayer, yet he has not freely given up his personal "rights" in

order to follow Jesus. He still wants his freedoms (which are counterfeit) along with the benefits of salvation. You cannot have both!"

"Unfortunately, we mostly quote such scriptures as, "If you confess with your mouth the Lord Jesus and believe in your heart that God has raised Him from the dead, you will be saved" (Romans 10:9). We tell people all they have to do is recite the magical prayer and they're in. But why don't we heed and teach Jesus' own words? He said, "But why do you call Me, 'Lord, Lord' and not do the things which I say?" (Luke 6:46) As we've seen, Lord means supreme master."

Yes, making Jesus our Lord does mean we surrender to Him *completely*. Yet, this is foundational to our beliefs and a biblical principle to our faith in Christ.

As the Western Church we have become focused on making members instead of cultivating converted *disciples*. His original followers and the people in the Scriptures are there as an example. We learn from their mistakes and how to strive to live a surrendered life to God through a firm and deep relationship with Him.

At the church on that Wednesday night, God spoke so clearly to me, "You lived your dream for one year, now it's time to live mine!"

I knew I couldn't argue with that. I had a choice to make though. Did I want to surrender to what His dream could possibly be or would I try to make my own dreams happen? I believe He would have let me make that choice. But we all know I chose to trust Him and His plan for me, and truly surrender. It was truly a painful and humbling process, but it has been so worth it!

It's all about surrender at the moment our soul cries out; and surrender *every day* until we get to be with our Creator in Heaven.

A favorite devotional read of mine is: Oswald Chambers: **My Utmost for His Highest**. He describes sanctification as death to self; being stripped of all identities (mother, wife, sister, brother etc.) and just being 'naked' before God. He quotes *Luke 14:26 "If anyone comes to Me and does not hate… his own life… he cannot be My disciple".*

I love how bluntly he puts sanctification next: *"We say, 'but this is so strict. Surely He does not require that of me.' Our Lord is strict, and He does require that of us. . . When I pray 'Lord, show me what sanctification means for me,' He will show me. It means being made one with Jesus.*

Sanctification is not something Jesus puts in me—it is Himself in me (see 1 Corinthians 1:30)."

Notice how Oswald refers to sanctification, or total surrender, as being made one with Jesus: intimacy. Intimacy is the key to a victorious faith, and through our journey and process, we become more and more one with Him just as Jesus is one with The Father.

The Mark of Moses...

Sometimes we question God if He really knows what He is doing. Moses questioned The Lord when he saw that Pharaohs' heart was too hard and the Israelites were still not delivered like The Lord had promised.

Don't we get impatient with the process sometimes? 'Lord, I thought you were doing this great thing, but it's looking worse now that I've begun my journey.'
Moses became frustrated, because he had a view of trying to free God's people with his own words, in his own strength. But God was going to deliver them with His own powerful hand.
Are you like Moses? In the middle of your calling, but feeling like it's not working, like something is off? Keep going; keep pursuing God and His vision for your life. If you are off kilter, allow God to straighten your path. We must choose to hear God's voice clearly and follow His direction, not simply what looks good in front of us. Moses had to be humbled, and learn to follow The Lord's voice exactly. Once He fully surrendered, God began to move powerfully. We need to remember that surrender to God's process is key to enduring the journey faithfully.

And Moses did just as The Lord commanded…

Let's Pray

Lord, help us go from vulnerable, broken people, to joyful and hopeful saints, and stay on a path of continual *surrender*. Let us not be afraid of surrender, for you are not a man that changes, or harms us. You are The One and Only. The loving Creator Who loved us so dearly you allowed Your only Son to take on the punishment that should've been ours. You sacrificed everything for us; help us, out of love, to sacrifice our selfishness for You, because you are more than deserving of that. Lord help us to surrender and set apart our minds, thoughts, hearts, our bodies, our families, ministries, careers, friends, and agendas.

Lord, any area we are holding onto with hesitation of You having Your way, soften our hearts so we would let it go, and allow you to come in and rearrange. For Your ways are higher than our ways, and Your thoughts are higher than our thoughts. Crucify our flesh, and help us to walk in the Spirit so that we may live a life of abundance in every aspect of the word. May we bring glory to You Who is worthy.

Lord have mercy on us, thank you for your kindness and patience; please make us a surrendering people. A people who desire to set apart our hearts and lives for The King of Kings. Lord, sanctify us. In Your holy name we pray. Amen.

Reflect

What areas have you felt a nudge or a gut instinct to let go of?

Is there something that keeps pulling you down in your life, or continues to send you spiraling in a direction you don't want to go?

Have you felt in your heart the call to surrender a specific action or way of thinking?

What area is next on God's list for you to surrender to Him?

What do you think you could be set free from if you surrender that thing to Him?

Sit and truly reflect: what place does God have on your *own* value list?

If God does not have the very *first* place above family, friends, career, etc. why not?

Repentance

"Repentance is a mark of intimacy with Me"

*A mark of intimacy is turning back to God, which is the **fulfillment of true Surrender**. When we truly surrender, repent and fully turn back to God, we are letting go of everything that is not of Him. By doing this we are taking a hold of everything that He has for us.*

There is a freedom in surrender, but once we let go, the void left would quickly be filled with even more to release if we didn't turn back to God. He is the only one who can heal the hurting areas in the deepest parts of our hearts and souls. That can only be accomplished when fulfilling the act of surrender by turning away from the path that led us to hurt, destruction, or pain, and allowing Him to heal us, comfort us, cleanse us, and change us.

Moses obeyed The Lord despite his weaknesses or insecurities. He repented of the excuses he gave to The Lord and the mindset that he was the wrong choice, and allowed God to use him. He also repented on behalf of Israel repeatedly as an intercessor. He begged God to forgive the nation of Israel for the wickedness they continued to commit time and time again.

Repentance should be a continuous lifestyle among believers, because as humans we are innately faulty, and in our life journey we are going from glory to glory. If we aren't repenting of a behavior, attitude, heart condition, or something that isn't in alignment with how Jesus would be acting, then we need to check ourselves.

I have gained the conviction that each day I need to pray God would crucify my flesh, and help me to walk in The Spirit. The times when I feel my flesh start to rise up, I have noticed that if I allow it to continue, things don't go so well. The days that are especially hard, are days I am *not* praying this, and *not* asking God to help me. As soon as I began to respond to the conviction to do as Paul says and 'crucify my flesh', I noticed immediately my mind becomes renewed by His Word. I can almost feel the icky flesh melt off my soul when I refocus and allow His Holy Spirit to work in me in that moment of frustration or whatever is trying to rise up against me.

There have been days where I'm wondering what in the world happened in my home, why is there strife, or chaos, or attitudes? Sometimes it will go on for a few days, and then I will take a breath, and look inward and say, "Oh, Lord, crucify *my* flesh. Help me to walk in the Spirit…" Now, I am not saying all the strife is because I'm walking around sinning and it's all my fault. However, I am saying that we have been given the power to change the atmosphere in our home, office, or wherever we may be, by simply turning our heart to God, and asking Him to live and move and breathe through us.

We find victory when we fully surrender and turn *toward* God and *away* from our flesh. He can then have jurisdiction to use us as broken vessels. If sin is abiding in our hearts, or being left there unrepented of, He cannot richly dwell in our hearts. Where rebellion is already abiding, His holy presence cannot dually dwell.

He is a holy God, and He loves us fiercely. He deserves to have us turn away from the behaviors, attitudes, and ways of our old selves. Paul says that the old man should be done away with, it should *die*… and the new man should come forth (2 Corinthians 5:17).

When I was about 19, I heard the gospel delivered in a way that I never had before. I truly heard how much God loved *me*. People can say 'Jesus loves you', but there is something about having a true revelation of how much He actually loves us as an individual, that can change *everything*; and that is exactly what happened to me.

At the time, my identity was wrapped up in another person, and *that* is unhealthy in and of itself. Add on deep undetectable pain accompanied by a lack of not knowing who I really was. When this relationship fell apart, it drove me to stuff the heartache down deep inside using alcohol, attention grabbing and completely living for myself.

For a lot of people, this behavior was typical, because, well it was college. However, it was the way I was abusing myself, the way I was being reckless with my own heart, body, mind, and soul, that was dangerous. Once I heard how much He loved me - that He saw everything I had ever done. He was there with me the nights that I was drinking just to become numb to my emotion. He was there with me the nights that I would take shots before I'd leave my dorm room, head out with a mixed drink, and shamelessly flirt with any man who would give me his attention, along with his beer. He was there when I made huge mistakes, and He was there to help me *not* make even bigger ones (I can only believe looking back on how reckless I was being that He was protecting me in spite of my foolish behavior). But once I realized He was there, something inside of me broke a little. Well, maybe a lot.

"God, You saw me do all this? Why are you still here?" How humbled I was and how desperate for His wild love for me. How could He still want someone like me after all that I knew He had seen me done?

Let me pause for a moment here and say, friend. If you find yourself in this same place, you need to know that Jesus sees it all. All of your flaws, failures, hurts… and yet He passionately loves you and is calling you higher. He has a plan and a purpose for you. He truly loves you and wants to help you reach your full potential. Ok… back to my story.

It was then, that I had an encounter with God I will never forget. I was at a retreat that my classmate invited me to. It was in that place that I instantly made 50 new friends, who didn't judge me, who genuinely wanted to know me, and who were all so goofy, joyful, loving, and fun. We were having such a great time… without alcohol!

I truly did not know this existed. I thought everyone who had parties and had any fun at all had to have alcohol involved. Being submerged into this culture was a radical awakening for me. I realized I had a *choice* to experience a different life.

And then He spoke to me in a way I had never heard before. It was at the end of one of the nights at the retreat. A woman had given a message, and afterward had prayed for us. During her closing, The Lord gave her a word of knowledge, and she very clearly spoke "someone in here needs to stop drinking!" I'm sure there were a few others that could've needed to hear that, but it truly felt like I was the only one in the room! I was exposed. God was calling me out!

The strange thing is, I didn't feel exposed in a bad way, I didn't feel shame, and I didn't feel judged. I felt love. I felt the love of The Father saying to me, "You are better than this, Crystal. You were created for more than living like this. Just stop. I have something so much better."

At that point I stopped. How could I continue after encountering His love in this wonderful way? It was really difficult socially, because I felt the need to let go of all of the ways I had been spending time with my friends. It felt weird. But I couldn't ignore the voice I so clearly heard and the love from the heart I felt it from. I didn't excommunicate my friends or I didn't try to. I just knew I couldn't be going to parties with them, because it was too big of a temptation, and after my encounter with God, it felt wrong and even awkward to be in that kind of environment. Honestly, even the smell of hard alcohol after this encounter made my stomach turn, and I couldn't even drink a drop of alcohol.

I had never felt so free, as when I let that lifestyle go and embraced His new life for me. God ended up showing me in His Word that He knew all about people getting drunk. He knew about hangovers, mistakes we make when drinking or mistakes we make when letting our emotions or anger control us; this isn't anything new. I was actually surprised-- but God is surprising sometimes. Who am I kidding?! After following Him for over a decade He still surprises me! God is not boring!

However, despite my being completely free for about 7 years, I did mess up a couple of times. Later on, after my relationship with Jesus had grown, I backslid. I let things go, and wasn't dealing with my emotions the right way, and turned to alcohol again. Waking up with a hangover was on thing but the weight of my sin had never felt so heavy. Honestly, I think once we know the truth and we turn back, the weight of the sin we carry becomes even heavier than ever because we have willfully turned away from the Truth. *(Hebrews 10:26)*

But there was that Love, sitting right there, waiting for me to turn right back to Him. I didn't need more than a couple reminders from God that alcohol was *not* for me, to get the message through. I don't need it. I need Him. And I've proven that to myself. It is unfortunate, but at the same time, I'm thankful to have learned my lesson, in hopes to help others, maybe even you.

Drunkenness is not honoring to God. *Anything* in excess pertaining to our *flesh* is not honoring to God. We need to possess the fruit of self-control. Even though alcohol is very socially acceptable even among Christians these days, I will be the "odd" one out and say, I've never felt freer than to just *not* have that be a part of our daily lives as a family. Drinking was never a part of my husband's life, and that was something that helped keep me accountable and also showed me that it is okay to have a conviction and follow it and not worry about the pressures of fitting in.

Am I saying alcohol is evil? No. This is *not* a debate on rules to follow, this is about surrender and repenting from what God personally convicts us of and being obedient to where God is calling us.

It is the *heart* behind the *use* of *anything* that matters to God most. Food, people, social media, alcohol. If we are using or abusing anything for a selfish gain or to fit in, our motives are wrong.

As followers of Christ we don't need to fit in. We need to obey God. If He has told us to stop, we need to simply just obey. The freedom of obedience is far better than a fleeting feeling of "fun" or fitting in.

In Romans it says that we should just not do the thing we aren't sure about because it is counted as sin.

"…If you do anything you believe is not right, you are sinning" Romans 14:23

It's not being a "prude" to abstain from things if you feel convicted to do so. It is honoring to the One Who matters most. Is drinking evil? No. Drunkenness is sin; that is clear in the Scripture. I had to ask myself "has there ever been *good* fruit from me being drunk?" The answer is *of course not*.

It is a matter of conviction to abstain from certain things as a follower. It is not a *salvation determination*, but a matter of one's journey to be more like Jesus; our journey to holiness. Our journey to be closer to Him. So let us not condemn one another as believers one way or the other *(Romans 2)*. But let us to strive to be *countercultural* verses a subculture of the world.

Repentance is a turning away from ourselves and turning to Jesus, Who is the Author and Finisher of our faith. Oswald Chambers says that "Sanctification is an impartation, not an imitation." He explains that it isn't necessarily drawing the power from Jesus to be holy, but it is drawing the actual holiness that was exhibited in Him, through myself.

There is strength in repenting. There is strength in turning to God's ways instead of our own. Our own lusts and desires will profit us nothing. But my obedience to take a hold of God's voice when He called me out of living like how I used to, has actually helped bring freedom to others who have struggled in similar areas.

God has anointed us to set the captives free and how can we do that if we too, are bound up just like the world; in the same sin and same life? To live a life that says: "We're the same, I just said the prayer, and that's all you need" is the weakest kind of faith. Paul said, *"Should we continue to live in sin so that God's grace may abound?* **GOD FORBID***!" (Romans 6:1)*

In Hebrew, "God forbid" means *"You cannot!"* Or *"Absolutely not!"*

When I've made the choice to heed to God's voice and repent, I always feel stronger. There is *power* when we *refuse* our flesh and *choose* to walk in The Spirit, and live as Jesus lived. He said we should become one with Him, just as He is One with The Father. He said that He did what The Father was doing, and that we should do the same.

Have you ever had *one of those days* where small irritating moments seem to build? One after another they dig at you. In my own life ,when a situation has the potential to become escalated, it is the times when I stop, breathe, pray and ask The Lord to crucify my flesh that I see a supernatural shift in the atmosphere. I watch God transform the situation right before my eyes. Now, there are other times where it is clear that I need to go to battle for my soul, my marriage, my family etc. Sometimes there are demonic forces that are trying to meddle with our lives. The Bible says that we do not war against flesh and blood but against principalities and powers of darkness. *(Ephesians 6:12)* But I believe a more in depth talk on this is for another book.

Doing whatever we want, or whatever makes us 'feel good' is not what God is doing. He is loving people, setting captives free, encouraging people, strengthening people, and He has called us to be salt and to be light in this earth as long as we are here. We are to be a seasoning, something to draw out the flavor of God's way of life among the darkness that surrounds us in this present time. Now, *that* is power! To have the very power and presence of God so within you that it can drive out darkness, and bring flavor and richness to a life that was bland and headed for destruction.

> "... We are to be a seasoning, something to draw out the flavor of God's way of life...."

Jesus said we should not be hidden like a lamp under a bush, but exposed, shining bright like a city on a hill (Matthew 5:14). If we match the shades of the world, how can we stand out as a shining city on a hill? It is time for us to step out in faith, and stand out. To be in this world, but not of it.

Sometimes, we want to change desperately. We want to turn away from our sin and the life we've been living when we discover how poisonous it is, but we feel helpless. Let me tell you right now, that God has given us every tool we need (2 Peter 1:3). God's grace is there for us!

Many think of God's grace as a cover for our sin, however, the true meaning of grace is actually the *empowerment from God Himself to overcome* our sin. What is holding us back from Him? We must turn from it for good. We have been given all authority over the power of the enemy and nothing shall by any means harm us. *(Luke 10:19)*

In 2 Corinthians 12:9 it says, "My *grace* is sufficient for you, for My ***power*** is made perfect in weakness (your human inability)." Peter says, "*Grace* be multiplied to you… as His divine ***power*** has given to us everything we need for living a godly life." (2 Peter 1:2-3) "… let us have ***grace***, by which we may ***serve*** God acceptably." (Hebrews 12:28). Notice how the words power and serve are used when talking about the ability to overcome when mentioning *grace*.

Grace is the free gift of God, and also the *empowerment* to *serve* God.

The Greek word for power is **Dunamis**, which means strength, power, and ability.

According to Strong's Concordance: The Greek word for grace is **Charis**: "Gift, favor, benefit… *the divine influence upon the heart*, and its *reflection* in the life" *an outward reflection of what is done in the heart*. A reflection of God's ways in our daily lives.

So, really when we break it down Grace is *God's influence* upon our hearts. His grace influences our heart motives and gives us the dynamite power to break through chains in our lives and move onward and upward as people of God! That's grace!

So when we are called to repentance but struggle, it is because we are 'falling short of the grace of God" … (Hebrews 12:15) Again, not His free gift of salvation, but His ability to help us out of the trouble!

So my encouragement to you is to take a hold of repentance by God's grace, because in our own human efforts we *will* fall short. However, God's grace ***is*** sufficient for us to embrace repentance! With Him *all* things are possible! Take heart, and turn fully to Christ Who is waiting to help you walk in a new way!

So we keep on praying for you, asking our God to enable you to live a life worthy of His call. May He give you the <u>power</u> to accomplish all the good things your faith prompts you to do. Then the name of our Lord Jesus will be honored because of the way you live, and you will be honored along with Him. This is all made possible because of the <u>grace</u> of our God and Lord, Jesus Christ.
2 Thessalonians 1:11-12

The Mark of Moses...

Why did the Lord take them on the scenic route to the Promised Land?

He knew the hearts of the people; He knew if He led them straight to the promises they would immediately forget all about Him. The purpose of the journey was so they could have opportunity to get to know Him deeper and build a relationship with Him.

Moses seemed to be the only one out of an entire nation that truly understood and desired this.

Truly, I think a huge mistake we make is forgetting that, although God is mighty, and knows all things, He still has emotion! He created emotion!

He feels!

Jesus wept and mourned. And just as the Israelites did, we can provoke Him to jealousy and even anger when we refuse and rebel and continue to be stubborn in our own ways.

When the Israelites so quickly turned their back on God and created a golden calf to worship, we see in a more intense way that God has emotion.

We see in this segment of scripture, that Moses' passion for The Lord was so fierce and intense. He couldn't stand to see the people hurting The Lord in such a way and he became greatly angered.

As an intercessor for the people, I believe Moses felt the Lord's pain and experienced a portion of The Lord's emotion.

When we sin, we need to understand we are hurting God's heart.

We are causing Him to be jealous, angry, hurt. That is why King David said, "oh Lord I have sinned against you." When he had committed a sin against another person. He understood God's emotion and His fierce passion for His people. He understood when he hurt someone by his sin, he also hurt The Lord.

Moses displays a sacrificial love when he pleads with The Lord to forgive the people's sin; but if not, to erase his name from God's book. I believe this kind of intercession shows that Moses *does* care about the people deeply. But even more so he cares about The Lord's heart for the people, and wants The Lord to preserve His promises.

He also displays a prophetic example of the heart of Christ; willing to take on the peoples' punishment for the love he knows The Father has for the people.

The wilderness is training ground to help us grow, turn our hearts *away* from ourselves and toward Him, so that we will not desire to go back to Egypt like the Israelites did (to go back to the world; back to the way we used to be.) Sometimes the desert is tough, and the journey is longer than we would like, but look around you! The Lord is showing Himself to be strong; we need only to ask Him to open our eyes.

He desires that you seek HIM instead of the promised land.

Let's Pray

Heavenly Father, thank you that it is your kindness that leads us to <u>repentance</u>. Your love is what You use to draw us *out* of darkness into Your marvelous light. Thank you that there is no condemnation in Christ Jesus, that You love us fiercely enough to call us away from darkness but that *same* love does not desire to accuse and condemn. You truly love with a perfect love, for You *are* love. Thank you for your grace that empowers us to change. I pray for your grace to flood each one reading this who has an area of change and repentance that needs to be made. Empower us Lord to turn to you, and leave sin behind us. I pray for deliverance for anyone who has struggled repeatedly with a certain nagging thing that will not seem to let go. Lord, break any chains from your people who desire to follow you, but are struggling with letting go. We bind the works of the devil and ask for your supernatural deliverance and freedom, in Jesus name. Lord have mercy and have Your way. Lead us to repentance Lord.

You said, 'If My people who are called by my name will humble themselves, and pray, and seek My face, and *turn from their wicked ways*, then I will hear from heaven and will forgive their sin and heal their land." (2 Chronicles 7:14). Lord help us to do these things so we can receive the healing that can only come from You. Help us to turn to you, not only in times of trouble, but as a lifestyle. I pray You would show people the goodness that is available as they abandon their own self will, surrender and turn toward you. In Jesus' Name.

Reflect

Have you only partially repented in any area you know needs to be changed? In what areas?

How have you fully repented, in action and thought?

What areas do you feel might need to be brought to the cross of Christ to inquire about repenting of?

What have you repented of in the past (actions, thoughts, or emotions) that you have seen fruit from?

Have you repented of something in the past but gone back to that thing?

Seek

"Seeking My face is a mark of intimacy with Me."

*When we **repent**, we turn from our own ideas of how things should look and begin to **seek** the only One Who can give us purpose, hope, and meaning.*

When we turn to Him, it doesn't end there; we need to *get to know* this Deliverer. Why does He care to deliver us? What is He like? Why does He love me like He does? What does He have for me that I don't already know about?

Moses sought God continually. He would climb a huge mountain to meet with The Lord face to face. He would spend 40 days and 40 nights at a time with The Lord. He would wait days just for The Lord's presence to manifest on the mountaintop. He pursued The Lord and His presence more than anything else in his life, and did God's will and accomplished many great things through his persistent seeking.

Seek first His kingdom and His righteousness and all these things will be added to you. (Matthew 6:33)

Seeking God is something I desire to continuously learn how to do, because our God is incomprehensible. Even the disciples who walked with and were friends with Jesus for 3 years straight, continued to say, "Who is this man?" …As we continue to seek Him we learn more about Him and His character, we learn about His many dimensions and we build a real relationship with Him based on trust. My desire is not only that we would continue to seek Him but that all followers would continually gain a hunger for searching Him out, and that it would *never* stop.

There are so many wonderful worship songs that beautifully describe seeking The Lord's face. One of my favorite Kari Jobe songs sings this: *"The more I seek you, the more I find you, the more I find you, the more I love you…"*

This is so very true for us as followers of Christ. As we continue to seek His face, and we continue to pursue knowing Him and His will, we truly will *find* Him. And just as spending time with a significant other will increase our fondness of that person and grow into deeper love and appreciation, so it is with our God.

He is a *relational* God! He desires companionship with us! The interesting thing to me is that as much as He desires to speak to us, He desires equally for us to speak to Him. As much as He desires to love on us, He desires for us to love Him. As He desires to be our helper, He desires for us to be His hands and feet and help Him accomplish His mission. He desires to be there for us and He equally desires for us to be there for Him. He desires to watch over us and He desires that we watch what He is doing. He desires to guide us just as He desires us to be willing to be led by Him.

Relationships in our everyday life are a two way street. They always take two people to make it work well. God designed relationship. How much more should we pour into the relationship with The One Who created us!?

I think it can be easy for us to take our relationship with Him for granted, because He is always there. He loves us unconditionally, we don't have to worry about His end of things, so we can oftentimes let things slide more easily. It's not entirely like a marriage because *He* is completely perfect! But He still desires our companionship. He desires to watch us grow in communion with Him and other people, so that we can flourish and become all that He has designed us to be.

Early on, when I was just getting to know The Lord, there was a vision I had during a worship song. As I closed my eyes it was like I was standing face to face with Jesus. It was as if I could see Him right before my eyes. When I was singing, it was like I wasn't just singing a song anymore; I was alone with Him in the room. It felt as though I was singing right to Him, and I could feel so much love emanating from His presence, I knew I would never be the same.

Recently, a song from a few years back really gripped my heart about knowing God face to face, called: You Won't Relent by Jesus Culture. This song incorporates a portion of the Song of Solomon from The Bible, which is a book that metaphorically describes the relationship between God and His people. There is one part of the song that sings, *"I don't want to talk about You, like You're not in the room; I wanna look right at You, I wanna sing right to You."*

When I heard that, it reminded me of the first time I had seen that picture of His love I previously shared, and these words have become my anthem attitude of worship for our King. My heart's desire is that every one of God's children would seek to experience intimate worship with Jesus in their own way. Worship is not limited to singing songs on a Sunday either. It comes in many forms of how we offer parts of our lives to Him: our finances, time, words or talent.

He is so incredible, because He knows exactly how we will relate with Him in the most special ways. Not every one person's experience will be the same; they will all be unique to each person because He is such an intimate and loving God- He knows how to speak to the depth of our hearts individually.

As we seek God for *Who He is*, instead of seeking Him for *what He can give us*, we encounter a heart change and a mind shift. Let me address this just a little bit further. You see, we come to know God as our Savior, our Provider, our Redeemer, our Healer, our Peace… but do we know Him as I AM? The previously mentioned characteristics of our God are incredible parts of our relationship with Him, but they are all based on <u>*what He does for me*</u>. **I AM** is based on how I know and love Him for simply, Who He Is. When we worship God for Who He Is, we are making a statement of: "I trust you because you are God and you are good." This was the first characteristic that God revealed to Moses and the one He referred to most of all.

When we struggle with feelings of insecurity or inferiority, God reminds us *Who He Is*. Who He is never changes. It is more powerful than anything He can *do* for us; not negating all that He has done for us, but *emphasizing* His complete deity as The Lord God

Almighty. We gain freedom from insecurity and inferiority when we understand that there is none like Him. He truly is The Living God and He is more than capable to do all that He has promised.

If I loved my spouse's backrubs or cooking, but only affirmed Him for giving me the best backrubs and making the best ribeye steak I've ever tasted; could it be that my love *may* be conditional? I would venture to think that it could turn into that if I wasn't careful.

The *position* of my spouse is *husband*, regardless of his excellent backrubs or tasty meals. His *behavior* that I love *stems from* the position he has in my heart and life. It is a product of his position. Our actions are the fruit of our relationship.

So let us differentiate in the same way with The Lord. Do I love Him for what He *does* for me? Or do I love Him for *Who* He Is?

Is it the *behavioral relationship* that I crave or the *positional relationship*? Both are there for a reason, but I believe it is essential we crave His positional relationship above the behavioral relationship. If we love God for what He does more than for Who He Is we can be in danger in the dry seasons.

*After we allow ourselves to become **vulnerable** with God; we give our **brokenness** to Him. We then receive the strength of **joy** that comes with the freedom from being broken and set free. From this joy we truly and fully **surrender**; and choose to **repent**. The intimacy only continues to build as we begin then to **seek** Him for Who He is; and not only for His blessings.*

Seeking God takes faith in Him, trust in His character, discipline regardless of circumstances, and perseverance. As a child of God, one of the hardest lessons I've learned, but one of the most vital for my relationship with God, is that life is more about our *journey* than us simply getting to the destination (heaven).

If it were not so, I would think we would simply say a formula prayer and enter into the pearly gates *immediately*. What would the point of *life* be, if not to *shape* us? And the shaping brings glory to God on earth to draw all men to Himself. Also to reconstruct us back into the original intended design He had for each of us so we can reign with Him for eternity.

God is using this life to shape us. He uses the pressures of our circumstances to help purify us. In James chapter 1 it says we should count it joy when we experience many different types of trials or temptations because we can be sure that the testing of our faith creates patience and endurance in us, and through this we become completely content in The Lord.

Consider this, could it be that it is about *How* we are being shaped for the work of the *destination*?

Heaven is not described in the Bible as a simple place in the sky to play a harp on a cloud- *(as seen on TV)*. There is so much in scripture that gives us glimpses not only into what Heaven is like, but we see how God operates. We can see patterns in the design of His creation and His desire for its purpose.

I believe Eternity is immensely more vast than we can comprehend. Apostle Paul says God transforms us and takes us from 'glory to glory'. So this would indicate we are not to stay the same as God finds us. We are to change. However, I believe that we are not changing for the sake of the people in the world or even for ourselves as much as we are changing to become increasingly more in unity with God's very nature. The goal is to become more and more like Christ. We are transformed into His likeness so that when we come into perfect fellowship with Him in Heaven, we can effectively do the work for His Kingdom on the other side.

This is something I had never really meditated on or searched the scriptures for until recently. There are things to be done in Heaven! I believe we will live life how it was originally intended before the fall of mankind. In Revelation it mentions the great city; The New Jerusalem which will be a perfect earth, how it was intended to be where King Jesus will reign.

If you are curious about Eternity, or find it difficult to think of Heaven or the afterlife being something other than a simple paradise or resting place, I would suggest reading *Driven By Eternity*, by *John Bevere*. He describes an excellent Biblical allegory of what it will be like to enter into Heaven and operate in our special gifts there! How exciting!

Jesus said, *"My Father is always working, and so am I"* *(John 5:17)*. It is in God's very nature to be at work and His desire for us is to serve one another with purpose and intention. If the Bible says God never changes, why would He stop working after His victory over Satan is complete in the last days?

In Revelation it *does* say there will be no more sorrow, crying, and pain in heaven, but it doesn't mention no more work. In chapter 22:3 it says, "His servants will serve Him." Some versions say 'worship Him'. Worship isn't mere singing songs to or about Him either. Worship is responding to His love in service, word, dance, song, any expression possible. The Weymouth New Testament even says, *"His servants will render Him holy service and will see His face…"* John is talking about what he is seeing in his vision of eternity. As we worship Him in spirit and in truth, we will see His face. And isn't this our goal? To know God face to face?

To *serve* means to be of assistance, to be of use; to work for; to perform the duties of a position or office.

If we consider that God is relational, we can gather that there will be much to accomplish there. There will be so many people to get to know, along with an infinite God and so many beautiful new displays of His perfect original intent for our lives.

When we look at God's character, He is a hard worker. He doesn't sleep. (Psalm 121:4) He established the world in 6 days and rested on the 7th. He works. And When He first created Adam; He placed him in charge over the entire earth. (Genesis 2:15) He intends for us to have purpose, regardless of our fallen state. There is work to be done. A Kingdom with no end. (Luke 1:33)

What is a kingdom? When we think of a kingdom in the earth, let's look at the definition: a *state* or *government* having a king or queen at its head.

State is defined as a unified people occupying a definite territory or nation. G*overnment* is described as the governing body of persons in a state or community; or direction over the actions of the ***citizens***.

We are also called Heavenly citizens *(Philippians 3:20 "…but our citizenship is in Heaven")*. We are meant to be citizens of a Kingdom that is not of this earth. So this means we are to be a unified people occupying Heaven and governing together in our heavenly community.

If we look at kingdoms in the realm of nature, there are different types of kingdoms: even in the animal kingdom there are categories, there are hierarchies, there are established duties. Even in the book of Proverbs (6:6), the wise Solomon tells us to look to the ant for its diligence. Compared to the animal kingdom, God's Kingdom is everlasting, and it is perfect. I believe there is and will be work to be done outside of this place called earth, and we should embrace every peak and valley as an opportunity of refinement for a greater purpose than we can even comprehend.

The Israelites went on a 40-year journey in the desert that should have physically taken them more like 11 days. Why? Because they were unwilling to let go of the things that God was asking them to. Their journey from God's perspective was more about getting "Egypt" out of them, and less about getting them out of Egypt. This brings me back to my point about our journey shaping us for the destination. The Israelites were not ready for the land flowing with milk and honey yet (which was a symbol of the afterlife); God needed to purify them, and was waiting for their hearts to turn toward Him fully. When we are glorified in the next life, we will be complete and whole; ready for the eternal duties that await us.

The wilderness times can be the most challenging times in our lives, but it is training ground, and we were made to be strong and courageous. I believe God draws us into the wilderness to strengthen us and train us for battle, and part of war is learning to withstand the blows given to us. The Bible says that a righteous man falls seven times, but he gets back up. *(Proverbs 24:16)*

When we receive forceful blows that the enemy means for our defeat; and yet we get back up, we are actually *resisting* the enemy! When we resist the devil the Word says he must flee!

Submit to God, resist the devil, and He will flee (James 4:7)

When Jesus would do incredible miracles, He was always spending time with The Father alone beforehand. He knew where His training ground was, and He went there willingly, and obediently, and when He emerged from the wilderness He was even more in tune with The Father, and able to continuously walk in the power of God.

We see a picture of the first time Jesus went into the wilderness, before He performed any miracles or did any wonders. He was met there by Satan himself, was tested, tempted and He overcame by the Word of God and resisting the devil. After His testing He began traveling throughout different regions preaching and healing 'every kind of disease and illness'. (Matthew 4:23)

After He hears about the beheading of His beloved friend, John the Baptist, Jesus goes off to be alone, but soon a crowd follows Him and He begins teaching; that is when the miracle of feeding the five thousand happens.

We shouldn't try to avoid or resist the desert times, the wilderness, or the trying times. As my Pastor always says, we need to *embrace* where we are on the way to where we are going.

In Philippians 4:13, Paul says he learned to be content no matter what his circumstances were, because he could do all things through Christ Who strengthened him. It will profit us nothing, if while we are in the wilderness, we complain, and wish we could go back to our old way of life like the Israelites did. If we choose the path of being discontent, we will take the long way around. There are no short cuts when we grow closer to God and allow Him to refine us; however, there is a path of least resistance.

When we stop resisting God and instead, begin to resist the *devil* and our flesh, we allow God to have His way. The journey becomes enjoyable, profitable, and we gain an intimacy with Him. This is an intimacy we gain as we build such an unwavering amount of trust in His character and Who He is. It makes our faith grow increasingly stronger.

There are also times when prayers aren't answered how we had thought, or maybe we are in a season of waiting, and we can start to lose hope. Sometimes these seasons make us look at Christ and say, "Who is He?" We can all go through seasons where we question Him and wonder if He is who we think He is.

Sometimes we are a lot like the disciples who didn't even recognize Jesus who was walking on the water while they were suffering a storm in their own boat. Their minds could not possibly wrap around the fact that Jesus was actually walking on the water. They could only come up with an explanation of "it must be a ghost!"

Why do we do that as humans? When God reveals Himself in an unfamiliar way, why do we try to explain it away with something that is *cultural* rather than *spiritual*? We try to justify something in a completely irrational way, because our finite minds cannot possibly comprehend the absolute deity and authority that God commands over the winds and waves in our lives.

One of the best pieces of wisdom I've ever received from my Pastor was this: To seek God's best for my life, and not merely things that *look* good or *feel* good, but to pray and seek His face to determine His will. To become so in tune with His voice, and His will that I can walk confidently with Him. Just like Jesus said, He sees what The Father is doing and we are supposed to do the same. Just because it is a *good* thing, doesn't mean it is a *God* thing, even in ministry. I've seen people get burnt out quick because they were doing what someone else *thought* they'd be good at, instead of where The Holy Spirit was leading with a "Yes!" and His favor.

In fact, I've *experienced* this. I love to serve. I love to help anywhere that I am needed. I am a natural leader, but if somebody needs help, tell me what you need and I'll help make it happen!

I was a part of a small but growing church, and was eager to watch God build it and make great things happen! I was serving anywhere that I could, but it wasn't much longer than a year after its birth that my husband felt we were being called to leave. Of course, I thought this was just due to his stinky attitude, and thought there must be enemy opposition to us being there! How could we possibly leave these people?! They were our family, and I was fully invested in the vision, and devoting time and effort there. There was just one problem…. Well maybe a couple. But the main problem was that my husband and I were not in unity. After a few years of marriage and some good godly council, I learned that unity is pretty important when trying to function and cultivate a healthy marriage.

When I found out that my husband was experiencing unrest, did I seek God, pray and listen to his concerns or care about his leading? Unfortunately, no. All I could think about was what a *grump* he was, and how he couldn't possibly be right about us needing to pray about leaving, or the possibility that God would be leading us out of that place (…boy was I stubborn).

The second problem was that I was burning myself out at both ends. I was trying to fill any and every role I possibly could, to try and please *people*, and I was letting people down in the process, because I didn't have enough time, or grace to do all that I was trying to do. I hadn't prayed about where I was supposed to serve, and at what capacity. I hadn't even *asked* God, I just 'knew it was the right thing to do', and went ahead and walked along my own path, instead of seeking His will to be sure it was in alignment with God's plans.

Looking back, there were many things God was trying to use to lead me on from that place and into the next place where He was calling. Sometimes we are just too stubborn, and at times we can't even fathom that God would cause such a shift in our lives. If it is good, it *has* to be from God, right? Well, not necessarily.

When I think about that specific time in our lives, there were a culmination of events which took place that led to us finally have to leave; I couldn't ignore God any longer. I joke about our experience saying God literally had to flush us out of there, because I wasn't going to leave! I loved those people, I still do, but I would've stubbornly stayed and fought to stay there if God hadn't intervened.

The next place we would go would be a place of much healing and growth. God used that place to open the windows of heaven to allow people in my life that would have never come in, had I not had God's hand on my life and listened to Him. My husband and I have experienced so much restorative growth in that following season, and came into unity like never before. God had led us into deeper unity in our marriage, in The Body of Christ, and with Him in a whole new way.

I am so thankful for the seemingly disruptive journeys that we get to go on with Jesus. Though, in the beginning there can be a lack of understanding and some heartache involved; because like little children we say, "but why Daddy?" Through our transition seasons in life that we weren't quite expecting, I can see how my husband has flourished in his different gifts and grown because of the difficult times. We have been able to be used by God in *new* ways.

God leads us out of places and into the new places of promise; it is part of our journey. When The Lord led us to leave our church family, as difficult as it was; it was one instance where I did not recognize my Lord and what He was doing, but now I've learned from it. I've learned how vital unity is with my husband, and how to trust his leading, and listen to his concerns. I've learned to pray about *everything* before I act. Sometimes I say things I shouldn't or make mistakes, like we all do, but I'm *working* on it!

For many years I longed for a godly woman to mentor me. Someone who had gone before; prayed through hard things, spent time with God; someone who could help me grow stronger in my faith. I was blessed in certain seasons to have mother or sister figures that loved me, prayed with me and helped lead me. But they were there for a season and I found myself in a sort of spiritual desert where there wasn't anyone really pouring into me on a continual basis. I had days where I felt discouraged and even defeated because I longed for someone to come alongside me and breathe God's life into me, personally. Going to church is great, but having a brother or sister deeply invested in our lives is a powerful tool God has given us.

Maybe you are in this season; wondering when you will have your Elijah? (Your godly mentor or person who can help guide you in your faith).

When will you have someone who has gone before you, who can pray for you, with you, encourage you, and help you grow, be there for you to support you, love you, and cheer you on?

I pray you dig into God while you wait. At the proper time The Lord will bring you that person or those people. I've been blessed to have some wonderful godly women come along side me to help sharpen me, encourage me, and help me grow. I believe that my season of waiting was a time of preparation and once I dug deeper into God and became content with allowing *Him* to teach me, encourage me and mentor me; that's when He blessed me with some extremely key people in my life.

Over the years on my journey with God, I have learned different ways in which I develop closeness with Jesus, and learn to hear His whisper. I first heard it through His Word when I was a teenager. I remember dealing with a lot of feelings of depression, anxiety, and self-hatred at the time. Honestly, I'm not really sure why; there was nothing much going on externally in my life at the time. But I did have a lot of self-condemnation, shame, and insecurity.

One day as I sat in my room as a teenage Catholic girl, I suddenly became overwhelmed with sadness and weeping. I began to have thoughts of self-hatred, and even self-injury. I felt an urge to take the screwdriver from my nightstand and begin to carve the word

"HATE" on my hand. As I tearfully began to scratch the back of my hand, a shift in the atmosphere came over me, and I felt love come into the room. It was almost as if I heard Love say, 'pick up your Bible'… I had never opened my Bible that I received from confirmation just a year before, but I felt the need to at that moment. When I opened it up, Psalm 138 said to me:

"In the day when I cried out, You answered me, and made me bold with strength in my soul…Though the Lord is on high, yet He regards the lowly; but the proud He knows from afar. Though I walk in the midst of trouble, you will revive me; You will stretch out your hand against the wrath of my enemies and Your right hand will save me. The Lord will perfect that which concerns me; Your mercy, O Lord endures forever; do not forsake the works of Your hands."…

It was the first time I heard God's voice, and now I know it was the first intense battle for my soul that I experienced before I even truly knew Christ…

A wonderful truth I have learned since then is that God is infinitely greater than anything Satan can throw at us. The truth is they are *NOT* counterparts or equal opposites! Satan is a <u>*created*</u> being; by the all-powerful Creator- **God**. None can compare to God! So often we can feel powerless, defeated, or hopeless when circumstances weigh on us.

I think what is even worse is when we *accept* what Satan throws at us as truth. Another powerful reality I know now is that I have always been a target of the enemy of my soul. We are all targets. I believe Satan sees the greatness God infuses in our souls and if he can try to position any hindrances along our path, he will do so. We have an enemy that *hates* us, and is constantly on mission to squeeze every drop of life out of us. He sees that God has a plan for our lives and that we are a severe potential threat to his kingdom of darkness. His goal is to steal from us, kill our joy and our spirit and try to destroy us and our calling. As we awaken, he is threatened by us; let us be aware of him and his tactics and do not allow him any foothold. *(Ephesians 4:27)*

I know now, that the flood of harmful and hateful thoughts I was experiencing was an attack from the enemy. Satan himself. It was also the first time I had ever felt like God was looking at me and speaking *right* to me. It was a supernatural battle for my soul and I knew God was fighting for me. It wouldn't be until years later that I would come to know Him more and start to seek Him in His Word.

However, He laid a foundation that night in a bold statement of: *"I AM here...I see you...I will help you..."* I truly heard His voice for the first time. I love that He uses His Word to speak directly to us. If you ever feel dry remember that His living Word is living water for our souls.

"For I hold you by your right hand— I, The Lord your God. And I say to you, 'Don't be afraid. I am here to help you.'" Isaiah 41:13

I heard His voice again, like I've shared previously, through the preacher who shared at the college retreat I attended. That night God spoke to my heart *"You are made for more."*

I heard Him through worship; seeing Him face to face was the beginning of Him using visions to speak to my heart, and show me prophetic things in my life. I heard Him say, *"Just seek My face."*

Now, I'm not sure if you know this or not, but I am a writer! I have inconsistently kept journals over the years, but more recently I have been much more diligent in keeping them regularly. The reason I've begun to be more consistent with my writing, is because as I have sat down to write more, I have begun to hear His voice more than ever before. It's as if the more I acknowledge what He's saying to me, the more He speaks.

When I write, I will sometimes praise Him, I will write prayers or I will write what I'm seeing God doing in my life currently. And many times, if I just sit in the quiet and spend time with Him, I can journal Him a question, pray, look in His Word, and suddenly… His answer comes in to my heart and onto the page before me. So I write what my heart 'hears' Him saying. If I *wait* on Him, He will speak to me, so journaling has become a most treasured time for me to spend with Jesus. Oftentimes as I write, I hear Him say, *"Listen, and I will speak…"* like His gentle, *"be still and know that I AM God."*

Another favorite thing I like to do to spend time with Jesus is have a prayer and soaking night. Soaking is something I only heard of in recent years, after my Pastor began holding prayer and soaking evenings in her home. It has truly been one of my favorite times to spend with Jesus. For those of you not quite familiar with what the term soaking is, it is simply soaking in His presence, just being. I think of being a teenage girl, and going to my best friend's house just because I wanted to be in her space. We would just sit there for hours and talk, or listen to music; it didn't really matter what we were doing as long as we were together. That is sort of how I think of soaking.

For example: On a typical prayer and soaking night, we would spend 3-4 hours in worship, prayer, reading His Word, maybe take communion, and just spend time privately mediating on Who God is. We would worship The Father, Jesus, and The Holy Spirit in our Pastor's home. But each night was different, because our Pastor would ask The Holy Spirit to lead, and it took a slightly different form each time. And each time there was a fresh revelation, and a different encounter with God. I heard Him more clearly during those times than any other time before in my life, and also had many instances of confirmation to prayers I had been writing down or silently praying. During these times I heard Him say, *"I want to spend time with you"*. What this really taught me is how greatly God wants time with us.

There are many ways we can spend time with The Lord, and seek Him. Everyone's relationship with Him is unique, so your connection and journey will look different than mine. However, seeking His face is probably one of the most important things we can ever do in our lifetime. Developing intimacy with our Creator is vital for our journey.

David was called a man after God's own heart (Acts 13:22). In Psalm 27:8 David says, *"When You said, 'Seek My face,' My heart said to You, 'Your face, Lord, I will seek.'"* Notice God desired for David to seek His face, not His hand, nor anything else about Him. Not His wisdom, glory, His face, He asked for intimacy.

> "Developing intimacy with our Creator is vital for our journey."

Victory through every battle we face stems from having intimacy with The Lord; it is truly the key to a victorious faith walk. David was a great example of a warrior for God. He was victorious in battle after battle because he would *listen* to the voice of God and was confident in his relationship with Him. He was close with God, and was a man after God's own heart. Reading the Psalms gives us a clear picture of how God was at the center of David's every thought and every part of his life. Even when he sinned, his thoughts were always turned toward God with a repentant heart.

We too can have victory in our battles as we continue to seek the face of God. Hearing His voice more clearly will cause us to have discernment to know how to fight our battles with wisdom, love, and power.

I encourage you to clear away distractions, and set aside entertainment for a moment. His great love for us deserves our attention. He has something fresh, something new for us, even today.

Let us dust off our Bibles, however long they have been left sitting; a day, a week, a month, a year. Seeking God is not only done in *our* way on *our* time; it is done in discipline, asking God how *He* desires for us to seek Him. He is not confined to our timeline either; we cannot become overly routine about how we spend time with The Lord.

I've learned this the hard way, because I liked how I was journaling or reading and hearing Him the way I was. It doesn't need to be exactly 60 minutes every morning at 5 am…Although I have found blessing in early morning sacrifice of my sleep and giving it to God. It can be 5 minutes at night before bed. The important factor is not the amount of time, or how much we read or pray, but it is vital to our faith health that we ask The Holy Spirit how *He* wants to spend time with us, and be willing to be flexible with His desires for us in that moment.

Are we willing to spend an hour when we were planning on 5 minutes? Or are we ok with having our 60 minutes interrupted by something that needs our attention? Will we be satisfied with the 5 minutes we had just sitting intentionally with Jesus? It's about the heart connecting with God and truly hearing Him.

God desires to be put first, above all else in our lives. I have never been disappointed when interrupting my busy schedule to be sure God has the utmost importance in my life when I hear Him asking for more time. Remember, The Lord *told* David *how* to seek Him. "*Seek My face*". When we do this, He will lead us into the time we spend with Him.

Does He want to show you something new in His Word? Does He have a song that He wants to use to minister to your heart? Does He want you to just be still? Does He want you to bring your heart to Him and just lay all your concerns at His feet? We must listen. That is what seeking His face is like. He cares what we would like to do with Him as well, but what an honor to hear how He wants to spend time with us and choose His way; the greatest blessings come from seeking God this way.

I am praying for a revival of a hunger and thirst for The Word of God among God's people. His Word is life, it is truth, it is alive, and active! It is exciting! If we aren't excited when reading the Bible; there is a lie that has been accepted in our hearts. I've been in that place! Where reading the Bible just didn't seem so interesting to me at the moment. But when I recognized that it was a lie, I decided it was time to pray and get to the bottom of this! Because, when I fight that thought and actually *read* my Bible, I'm always amazed at how God speaks to me!

Oswald Chambers says, "Staleness is an indication that something in our lives is out of step with God."

The times when I have been dry and stale feeling, bored with the Bible, or apathetic with my faith; I have always found that something was out of step in my mind or heart. Once I simply asked God to help me with this feeling and was honest with Him; the feeling would break off and I would find rejuvenation in His presence.

The Bible says that Jesus is the Word! It is yet another very vital aspect of how God connects with us. His Word is the map and instruction manual we need in order to be victorious in this life.

In Ephesians 6 it declares The Word of God is the Sword, the ***only*** offensive weapon we are given. How did Christ overcome the temptation of Satan? He repeatedly declared The Word of God.

Do not be deceived that it is boring or unimportant to read Gods Word. Do not be discouraged if it seems you aren't gaining understanding or if it seems it is too complex. I too, had that problem and I simply asked The Lord to help me understand and He of course was quick to answer that prayer! Do not place it aside as if it is an old historical manuscript void of power. That could not be *farther* from the truth. I urge you to pray and ask The Holy Spirit to refresh your faith; to bring excitement to your relationship with Him again; to bring to life His Word to you once again; and remove anything that is blocking you from receiving this exciting abundant life with Him. He does not wish to keep you at an arm's length but to draw you into His heart.

I want to share with you some facts about the Bible that I feel bring awe and excitement into our journeys and confirm not simply the validity of God's Word but the power!

1. The Bible was written over a 1500 year period by approximately 40 men of 3 different continents and all kinds of backgrounds (from fishermen and shepherds to military and doctors).- and yet it is completely cohesive

2. It is the only book which includes actual words of God- it is written more than 3,000 times "thus saith The Lord."

3. It is historically accurate- there were several secular historians who wrote about the events of the New Testament at the same time The Scripture was being written which backs up the accuracy of The Scriptures by men who would have nothing to gain. (Josephus & Tacitus were 2 main historians)

4. There are more than 3,200 verses with fulfilled prophecy written in The Bible.

5. There are over 300 prophecies written in the Old Testament (Torah) that speak of the coming Messiah and Jesus Christ fulfilled them _all_.
    a. The probability of one man fulfilling only 8 of these prophecies would be 1 in 10^{17} - if this were illustrated it would look like the entire state of Texas covered in silver dollars- 2 feet deep. One of those silver dollars has a mark. Someone being placed in a random spot and selecting one silver dollar and having it be the marked one is the probability of _only 8_ of these prophecies fulfilled. Yet Christ fulfilled all 300 of them.

The Mark of Moses...

Moses would meet with The Lord face to face in the "Tent of Meeting" as 'one speaks to a friend'.
The friendship they had is incredible, intimate and one of a kind. It shows the desire of God's heart to commune with His people, and it is due to the obedience in Moses' heart and his desire to please The Lord.
For the first time in the scriptures, it is revealed how deeply God desires to be approachable. That The Lord longs to talk with us face to face. And Moses models for us how we can have this throughout his own story.

Let's Pray

Father God, we love you so much. We're so thankful that You are a relational God, and not a God who is far off and disconnected. I know some people have possibly felt that way at times in their life, but I pray right now that you would minister to their hearts, and show them how deeply you love them. I pray for a revelation of your love to overcome them. I ask Lord, for you to put action to our faith. That seeking *You* and Your Kingdom first would become our hearts desire. As a deer pants for water, so our soul longs for You, Oh Lord.

Father, Your Word says, "Draw close to me and I will draw close to you". That is a promise, and You are not a man that you can lie. So help us to draw close to You, even when we don't feel like it, or even when we are hard pressed on every side. Help us to not grow weary in doing good, but to seek You, for at the proper season, we will reap a harvest if we do not give up.

Lord, show us how rewarding it is to seek Your face over Your hand. Help us to be a people whose souls long for you. As we seek You, may we find You; and as we find You, may we grow more deeply in love with You than we have ever dared to dream.

Help us to know You more, and develop a level of intimacy with You that surpasses every trouble or sorrow we've ever had or ever will have in this life. Develop in us a deeper understanding of Your heart, Your Word, Your truth, Your love, and Your presence. In Jesus' name.

Reflect

What are your favorite ways to seek God?

What could you try that would 'shake up' your time with God and how you spend it?

When you've been intentional about pursuing God and trying to know Him more, what benefits have you seen?

What have you heard God saying lately?

How can you try and hear His voice more clearly?

What is God saying even now? (try just being still and asking Him to speak... sometimes being still and waiting is needed in order to hear Him more clearly)

Walk

"Walking with Me, is a mark of intimacy with Me"

*When we begin to **walk** in our God-given purpose, it is a mark of intimacy with our Creator. When we truly **seek** God's face, we begin to desire God's will above our own more and more. When we seek and see God's will begin to manifest in our lives, we begin to discover more and more of our purpose, and can begin to **walk** it out with Him.*

    When we discover more about Him, then we can begin to walk *on* purpose, or intentionally, because we gain more and more of a sense *of* purpose. Our journey with God is not meant to be lived as a boring crutch, but rather a purposeful adventure full of life abundant!

    Many of the Israelites continued to complain to God and Moses about their trials during their 40 year journey through the wilderness. The Israelites deprived themselves of intimacy with God which created a lack of essential trust they needed to endure their circumstances with strength. However, Moses knew God face to face, and therefore, knew they could trust God regardless of the hardships of their journey.

    Sometimes, I think we get discouraged with the big questions, "What is my purpose?" "What is God's will?" If we get preoccupied with those questions, we can become stagnant, stale, reticent, or lazy because we don't know where to go next, or what to do.

A very freeing truth that God revealed to me is that He has laid the answers out in the Bible, if I would only take Him at His Word.

His purpose for us is: to seek first His Kingdom and righteousness (Matthew 6:33); to love The Lord my God with all my heart soul mind and strength (Luke 10:27); to do unto others as I would have them do to me (Luke 6:31); to forgive quickly so I may be forgiven (Matthew 6:14); to crucify my flesh, and walk in the spirit (Galatians 5:24); to be holy for He is holy (1 Peter 1:16, Leviticus 20:26); to shine like a city on a hill, and not hide my light from the world (Matthew 5:14); to live for Him unashamed (Romans 1:16); to stay connected to The Body of Christ (Hebrews 10:25); to pray without ceasing (1 Thessalonians 5:16-18); to abide in Him like Jesus did The Father (John 15:4); to put on the whole armor of God (Ephesians 6:11-18); to war in the spirit and not in the flesh (Ephesians 6:12); To know who our enemy is (2 Corinthians 10:3); ultimately it's to know Who our God is …. and *so* much more!

It is all laid out in His Word. If I have a question, I need to check my question with The Word of God, and it will be answered. Sometimes, our questions are not answered plainly, or how we think they should be answered. If we don't have a relationship with Jesus built on trust; because He is a good God Who loves us unconditionally, then it may prove to be tough to have our questions seemingly unanswered. It is in the waiting that our faith really gets tested. But rest assured, The Word also says that Jesus has given us peace, not as the world gives, but only as He can give; a peace that surpasses all understanding that will guard our hearts and minds in Christ Jesus. (John 14:27)

Sometimes we also get side tracked by thinking we need to find out what calling or vocation we are designed to have, because we tend to wrap our identity up in what we do; this is especially prevalent in our western culture. However, if we would fulfill God's purpose that I explained previously, then we would be so in tune with The Holy spirit that we would *find* the vision, vocation, or calling that God has for us. And we should hold loosely to the vocation because that is not necessarily our purpose or destiny; it is most likely a *tool* for our destiny. We live a walk, and on this side of eternity most of the value is in the *journey* not the *destination*. We are truly on a journey to become fit for the destination awaiting us.

> "We live a walk and on this side of eternity most of the value is in the journey not the destination."

We must walk by faith, and not by sight, as believers. Faith is the substance of things hoped for, the evidence of things not seen. (Hebrews 11:1) So, we must strive to walk honoring to God, regardless of what we see; according to our *hope* and not our circumstances.

As my Pastor always encourages me: circumstances are subject to change when God is involved. God has an amazing way of intervening in our circumstances when we trust Him, ask Him, and allow Him to move. Sometimes, I think we can hold Him back by being stubborn, disobedient or even doubtful.

I've seen evidence of this in my own life when I know The Lord has put on my heart to do something and I have been lazy about it, ignored it, or flat out refused to do what He was asking me to do. It is almost as if I can feel His hand of favor lift from me and once I repent and comply with His urging, the flow of favor comes back into my life. In those times I felt The Lord speaking right to my heart that if I were to just go back to the *last* thing that He instructed me to do, then He could give me my next step, full of favor and faith.

"You will be blessed if you obey the commands of The Lord your God..." Deuteronomy 11:27

There were times I was like a Jonah. The Lord would place something on my heart to do and I would protest. My protest was maybe less dramatic than skipping the country and trying to flee from God. But the heart was still the same. "Um, no thanks, Lord!".... or

"Not today." Either way, I wasn't acting upon the small stirring in my heart. Once I got tired of being in the belly of the whale, I would ask The Lord what was going on and He would quickly reveal to me that He had already impressed the next step upon my heart, I had yet to obey. God has been refining this gift in me over the years of discerning His still small voice. His voice that says, *"this is the way walk in it"* (Is. 30:21)

My family and I had made kind of a friend. A homeless man named Stephen. It began one day after a ministry event that I saw him as I was exiting the off ramp to go home. I happened to have a plate of left over fresh food with me in the car; it was given to me from the event earlier that day. I felt compelled by The Lord to offer it to this man. He was so grateful and elated and it was an absolute joy to chat with him. He thanked me repeatedly. I asked his name and that's when I became friends with Stephen. I knew I had to introduce my family to him; once in a while we would see him and God would instruct us to bring him certain items.

One day in particular my family and I were in a *huge* rush to go to a family function. The Lord had prompted me to bring along a bag of items for Stephen. But he was on the opposite side of the bridge that we were on and there wasn't a safe place to pull off, plus we were running late- like *really* late. I chose *not* to listen to the still small voice that grew louder and louder until it felt like a shout in my soul. I drove down the freeway with an urging in my spirit to turn around and repent from not heeding the voice I knew I had so clearly heard. For one fleeting moment I pondered the thought that I could try to justify to The Lord that I hadn't had time that day; surely God would understand the demands of making family happy… but as quickly as that thought bubble popped above my head, I burst it because I knew the truth. That thought was not God's thought. It was not His heart. I *had* to turn around. By this time I was already 10 minutes down the freeway the wrong way.

There is something refreshing about pleasing The Lord with our obedience and releasing the feeling of needing to please man. I told my husband the heavy burden on my heart and I am so very thankful for a godly husband. He encouraged me, as he always does, and told me if God said to do it- I'd better listen!

We turned around, pulled off the highway and there he was. So grateful to receive the offering we had for him that day. I do not say this to brag about our giving. In fact it is difficult for me to share this story because in Matthew 6:2-4 (paraphrased) it says when we give not to advertise it to get attention or praise. People like that are hypocrites and peoples praise becomes their reward. We are supposed to give in secret so our Father in Heaven will reward us. However, I share out of obedience. The Lord put this story on my heart to share because it's about walking in His way, hearing His still small voice and the importance of obeying. It's about walking in step with His Holy Spirit. As we walk with Him, others are blessed around us and we are blessed.

Do you feel dry or discouraged? When was the last time you heard God's voice? What did He tell you? (or have you not truly taken the time to listen?) Trust me. He longs for you to hear His voice. If God has given you an instruction and you have not followed through, I urge you to pray and obey. He will continue to guide you, but He needs an obedient heart that is pliable and workable in His hands. I say this because I know from experience. Your abundant life is waiting!

According to the Scripture we are to _walk_: blameless; pure; obedient; humbly; honestly; by faith; with integrity; in the light; with wise men; in newness of life; not after the flesh but after the Spirit; where He calls us (even through the valley of the shadow of death); on wings of eagles; worthy of our calling and walking worthy of God.

In the culture we live in, walking this way can be seemingly impossible. It can even seem so intimidating that we ignore it completely, or cherry pick what we think is the most *reasonable* thing for Him to ask of us. And we can have the mentality that if we do *some* of it, it's better than nothing. But God doesn't keep score. He simply asks of us, and His sacrifice demands our obedience. Our *whole* heart surrendered to Him, our full obedience.

I have been there. I have had my comfort zone of going to church on Sundays and reveling in my flesh Monday through Saturday. I have tried to fill myself up with positive things and throw in some scripture verses to make myself feel good, only to find myself feeling empty at the end of the day. I was filling myself with ideas, or things that made me feel good about *me*. This is a self-centered kind of faith not a Jesus centered faith. In reality, what I really needed was to be filled with God's Spirit, His love, His grace and His truth. I had years where I didn't walk after the Spirit but after my own flesh; I subtly lived a selfish Christian life.

Is that even a *real* thing? A selfish-Christian life? I'm pretty sure that's an oxymoron. The opposite of Christ Himself. It was me; I was the cherry-picker. I liked the salvation part but I didn't want the full obedience part, the whole "walking like Jesus walked" was tough work, and I'm not perfect; how could He possibly expect me to walk like that, right? But, you guys, I struggled in this state *so badly*. I would do certain "Christian" activities but go to church and feel like I needed to get saved all over again week after week. I remember breaking down and praying one time asking God to have mercy and not let me die in the state I was in, because I knew- deep down- I was wrong. I was living religiously and not in the freedom Christ wanted me to. In my soul, I sincerely knew something was missing. My 'religion' wasn't pure, it was selfish. I did things that made *me* happy, I did things to serve *my* wants, *my* needs, *my* flesh, and I didn't really look out for others.

Do you want to know what my problem was? It was all about me- I was doing everything in my own strength and not in the empowering grace God had for me.

Jesus died to cover our sins, to keep us from damnation. But what kind of life is it to live *just* so I don't go to hell? To abuse His grace? Paul said, should we continue to sin just so God's grace abounds? GOD FORBID…. Meaning ***ABSOLUTELY NOT!***

No… I want to be different. I've made up my mind. In a culture that says it's ok to do whatever makes me *feel* good, a culture that justifies its sin by gaining social media support, and a culture who doesn't like the words: sin, holy, obedience, sanctification, or the like. I want to be *all* that God has called me to be and I want to see a generation rise up and know the difference between legalism and holiness; a generation who wants to see grace being received and *used* to empower others, not *abuse* God.

I want to see a generation that does *not worry* whether others want to label them as legalistic or zealous. Because if we are obedient out of *love*, and we don't condemn others in the process of our becoming more and more holy or like Jesus, we will be blessed, and others will be blessed by us! In the end, we are only truly accountable to *One*, and that may be why a lot of people continue to practice sin without hesitation. But that is why I choose to try my best by God's grace to live holy for Him. He is Holy. He is Judge. He is $LOVE$. He is The Mighty King and I want to do my best to honor Him with every aspect of my life, thoughts, desires, and actions. It took a lot of breaking to get me to that point. I had to be ok with people not understanding my convictions, and I had to let go of people-pleasing and embrace God-pleasing.

This is a tough subject because everyone is on their own unique journey with The Lord, and it can be difficult to understand why someone feels convicted about abstaining from something that someone else considers completely fine. However, we cannot let our hearts be offended or confused. Seeking The Lord on our own is vital so we can ask Him and clearly hear what He has to say about our *own* walk when these questions come up. This is why The Word of God is so important.

We need to have understanding for one another and respect that everyone is on their own journey, while at the same time being unwavering in our obedience to God and what He is asking of us. And we need to seek God as King David did and ask the tough question: Lord, search me, and show me if there is any wicked way in me. (Psalm 139:24). In Hebrews 12:1 Paul said to strip off every weight that slows us down, especially the sin that so easily trips us up; and to run with endurance the race God has set before us. Our walk is a marathon and if there is anything in our life that hinders us, we should get it out of our lives (strip off the weight), because God and His purpose for us is more essential than a temporary satisfaction.

Imagine trying to efficiently and effectively run a marathon, but you are wearing a backpack full of bricks. These bricks have words on them: regret, shame, anger, unforgiveness ... you have shackles of lust around your ankles that trip you up every time you try to move forward. You have your cell phone out with hundreds of notifications, messages, alerts popping up and it makes you completely distracted from the path in front of you. It would be *impossible* to be efficient and *finish well* with these weights that so easily beset you. Pray about what weights God would have you cast off today. Am I saying a cell phone is sinful? No. However, God looks at the motives of the heart in all the things we do. We may not be intentionally sinning against God, but we must ask ourselves the question. Is this bringing me closer to Him or pulling me further away? Is this making me more like Christ, or more like myself? This isn't an easy question to ask ourselves, but it is necessary to dig deep and ask the tough questions as we climb the mountain to meet with God face-to-face.

The Mark of Moses...

Seek justice, love mercy, <u>walk</u> humbly with your God. (Micah 6:8)

Moses continually walked humbly with God until the very end of his life.
Numbers 12:3 states that Moses was more humble than any other person on earth.
The Lord hears the complaints of the people being jealous of Moses' relationship with Him and rebukes them saying, "Now listen… I would reveal myself in visions. I would speak in dreams… but not with my servant Moses. Of all my house, he is the one I trust. I speak to him face to face, clearly and not in riddles! He sees the Lord as He is…"
This is incredible. The Lord defends Moses as a *friend* (just as Moses defended God when the people turned to the golden calf), and shares with them *why* He has such a unique relationship with Him. He had trust. Moses was humble, obedient, and never turned away from God.

It was the <u>way</u> Moses walked that mattered the most. It was his heart motives. His heart was for God. He was motivated by love to walk pleasing to The Lord. The Israelites journeyed along with Moses and The Lord for those 40 years, but it was Moses that maintained an incredibly unique and close relationship with God.

Humble yourselves before the Lord and He will lift you up (James 4:10)

Anyone who wants to be greatest, must be last and servant of all (Mark 9:35)

For it is the one who is least among you all who is the greatest (Luke 9:48)

The one time that Moses actually disobeyed, he doesn't argue with The Lord about his punishment (not to enter the Promised Land). I picture in my mind that he takes the repercussion humbly because He knows The Lord, he knows He is holy, he knows The Lord is just in his decision, and he does truly revere and honor the Lord as a best friend.

When I looked at the end of Moses life, I saw a beautiful display of the result of walking intimately with The Lord. The scripture says, *"There has never been another prophet in Israel like Moses, whom the Lord knew face to face."* They spoke every day for most of Moses' adult life, face to face. Moses' burial place is a secret, only God knows where his body lies; God knows Moses' physical body is made from dust, yet, He doesn't dismiss the things that are temporal. He cares about the details of our lives, physically and spiritually.

Let's pray

Dear Lord, help us to *walk* worthy of the calling that You have placed on our lives (Ephesians 4:1). Forgive us for areas in which we have compromised, and help us to turn away from compromise, and into Your arms of love. Help us to receive Your love and kindness that draws us to repentance.

Let us too, be motivated by love to walk pleasing to The Lord. Help us to walk according to Your Word. We need You, O Lord in these desperate times. Let us be a generation marked with your holiness. Let us walk hard after You.

Help us to love you more than we love ourselves, and help us to check our hearts moment by moment, day by day so that our hearts do not wander and we do not stray away from You.

Lord, You have an adventure waiting for us, if we would just *walk* with You! I pray that you would help each of us to discover a greater adventure than what we have previously had. I ask for an added measure of faith, and obedience to come along with that.

I thank You, Lord for being a lamp unto our feet and guiding us on our walk with You, and I pray that we would not grow weary in doing good, for at the proper time, we will reap a harvest if we do not give up! (*Gal 6:9*) In Jesus' Name. Amen.

Reflect

Have you ever felt hung up on wondering what your purpose is because in your mind it has been related to your vocation? How?

How can you take your purpose "out of the box"? What do you think it could be if it's not limited to your job? (encourager, father/mother, warrior, nurturer etc.)

What questions do you have about your purpose?
Let's check it with The Word of God now. Check the concordance in the back of your Bible for key words, or even google "what does The Bible say about…"

If anything isn't in alignment with God's Word then it isn't God's best, have you ever been a part of something that you didn't feel was God's best?

The Bible says that there is no fear in love; that means we can rest in God, knowing we don't have to be fearful of what is to come.
Have you ever experienced fear surrounding the thought of asking God how He might be rearranging your life? (Don't let it hold you back!)

What are you afraid of? I encourage you to release it to Him now.

Most of the time worry, doubt or fear comes from our own flesh or lack of trust with God; or even sometimes from the enemy. God will send warnings, but His tone tends to be one, not of fear, but of love and concern.

Can you identify the voices of fear in your own life and where they are coming from?

What does the voice of fear say?

What does the voice of The Loving Father say?

FULFILL

"Fulfilling your destiny is a mark of intimacy with me"

A mark of intimacy with our Creator is when we discover how to **walk** in the purpose we find in Him. It is then that we begin to **fulfill** our destiny. When we see His vision and purpose for our lives and walk closely with Him; soon enough we look back and realize we are walking in and fulfilling our destiny.

We are all destined for greatness in Christ. God has a path and purpose for us to fulfill a destiny. Once we truly begin to seek God, and walk in the purposes He has called us to, we begin to fulfill our destiny, perhaps without even knowing it.

When I say "walk in the purposes God has called us to", my mind instantly thinks of how easily preoccupied we can become with the question of wondering *what* my purpose is. Like it is one huge feat to accomplish, and if we don't crack God's code, we will never fulfill what God's mission for our lives. Not only can this way of thinking about it be intimidating, but this can lead us to become stagnant if we feel we have no clue what our destiny or purpose could be. However, I tend to think of walking in God's purposes as a *daily adventure*. A daily purpose. Taking thousands of small obedient steps every day.

Fulfilling our destiny isn't necessarily in the *what*, but in the *Who*. If I am focused on the Who, He will help me walk that day to be the best parent I can be to my child. To smile at the soul that needs the warmth of Jesus' heart toward him. If I am focused on the *Who*, He will help me serve my family or church selflessly, and avoid trivial offenses or the feeling of being burnt out. If I am focused on the *Who*, He will guide my path that day, and might prompt me to take a new way to work, where I will be able to bless a hurting heart. If I am focused on the *Who*, I will become exceedingly in tune with His voice and will become more prompt in my obedience to His nudges. Then I will look back at the day in awe of each of the *many* purposes I did, in fact, fulfill that day.

Actually, we can look at Moses and erroneously only focus on the calling God placed on his life to help deliver Israel from Egypt (Which is a fantastically huge call). When, truly, it was the *daily* obedience Moses had; the "… and Moses did just as The Lord commanded…" that *added up* to the fulfilling of the call God placed on his life.

When The Lord told Moses what he was about to do, Moses freaked out, and was sure he was not the man for the job. Could it be that The Lord knows our response would be '*no way*' if we knew too much? Could it be that when He requests us for an extraordinary call that it is easier in our human nature to choose to *ignore* it? Perhaps sometimes, He simply requires our daily obedient steps in order to lead us to fulfill His call.

I encourage you to walk in small daily obedient steps with The Lord with the intention of making Him smile. You too, will look back and smile at all of the incredible ways God uses you to bless others in your every day. As we continue in this way of walking His plans will unfold for us and we will hear His call more clearly.

We see at the end of Moses' life that The Lord is faithful to show him the Promised Land, and that all of his hard work paid off. Indeed, he fulfilled what The Lord had purposed for him, and so much more than solely delivering Gods people. He gained the reward of knowing Almighty God and becoming a man who would be known to be one of the greatest prophets in all of Israel. The first to hear the name of YAHWEH; the one who knew God face-to-face, and the most humble man on the earth. The Lord could have used *anyone* to deliver the Israelites. He could have done it Himself. Instead He chose to *shape* Moses through the journey He called him to.

This shaping of Moses that took place still encourages us today as we look intently at his life and his relationship with The Living God. Looking with an eternal lens, the shaping of Moses was not just for him in his lifetime, but it goes on; it is an eternal shaping. As believers, our lives do not end on the earth. The earthly life we are given is a shaping and refining process for Eternity. It helps *my* earthly mind and my every day thought process to focus on that scriptural truth. It makes my life more exciting when I am walking in step with The Holy Spirit, asking Him who He wants to bless today and watching Him work through my broken self.

Living our life for eternity gives us a much broader perspective of purpose.

"Therefore, since we are receiving a kingdom, which cannot be shaken, let us have grace, by which we may serve God acceptably." (Hebrews 12:28)

We are *receiving* a kingdom; we will *reign* with Christ, so we are encouraged to *serve* Him here and now acceptably. How exciting to know we aren't finished at the end of our earthly life!

"Now every athlete who goes into training conducts himself temperately and restricts himself in all things. They do it to win a wreath that will soon wither, but we do it to receive a crown of eternal blessedness that cannot wither." (1 Corinthians 9:25)

This scripture again, points to eternal living and rewards. The way we live *here* will count in the life to come. We will have to stand before The Lord and give an account for our life, but the things we do for Him now will reap reward in the Heavenly Kingdom. Let us be a people with eternity focused purposes; fulfilling our call knowing we will be reaping eternal rewards.

In Ephesians 2:10 it says *"we are God's workmanship, created for good works in Christ Jesus."* The Greek word for workmanship is **poiema** – meaning we are skillfully and artfully created and are His poem; His masterpiece. We have been artfully created, as a poem, for good works in Christ. This means that we have a purpose; a destiny to fulfill. Not only does it mean that we have a purpose and a destiny, but that we have one that *only we* can fulfill. Our identity in Christ is as unique as our own fingerprint. If we can tap into the unique identity and destiny that we have, we will surly leave the mark of Jesus on the world around us, and impact generations to come.

Make no mistake that the *purpose* of our destiny we are called to is not *fulfilled* in us making the best life for *ourselves* that we possibly can. It also has little to do with living life just to be a good person and helping people around us philanthropically or otherwise, as good as that feels. This can be a difficult thing to grasp, especially in our culture where it is common to give to charity and do good. The Scripture says people will identify Christ in us by the *love* we carry. I aim to help us regain our focus on the main goal. It's *all* about knowing Jesus and making Him known!

> *"If we can tap into the unique identity and destiny that we have, we will surly leave the mark of Jesus on the world around us...."*

Will we experience a wonderful life, and help people in many ways along our journey? Absolutely! So, I'm not saying it is wrong to want to make a good life, be a good person, and help people. But if our *motive* is to make *ourselves* look good or feel good, we are missing the point. We should be aiming to make *Jesus* look good! We are called for more. We have a higher calling than we think. Living a *good* life is not enough. We need to live a *God* life. We need to move outside of ourselves. Jesus taught us to be completely selfless. He was fully man and fully God; who else has more reason to actually boast and make Himself look good? And yet, that is not His nature. He exemplified the opposite. Become the least and you shall be first. His teachings defy human nature and logic. Jesus was counter-cultural in His messages, which is why He was loved by some and hated by others.

Oswald Chambers talks about the rich young ruler in My Utmost for His Highest:

"Have you ever been speechless with sorrow?

'When he heard this, he became very sorrowful, for he was very rich.' (Luke 18:23)

Has God's Word ever come to you, pointing out an area of your life, requiring you to yield it to Him? Has He pointed out certain personal qualities, desires, and interests, or ... relationships...? "If you really mean what you say, these are the conditions" ... "Rid yourself - of everything - until you are a mere conscious human being standing before Him, and then give God that. What Jesus says is difficult. It is only easy when it is heard by those who have His nature in them. Discouragement is disillusioned self-love; and self-love may be love for my devotion to Jesus, not love for Jesus Himself."

Wow. Is my self-love truly love for Jesus Himself or is it love for my devotion to Jesus? I love contemplating the perspective of someone that challenges me. When I read the above section, I have to ponder deeply and ask Jesus for myself, "what have I not yielded to you, my Lord?" This is not an easy, fluffy thing to read for me; but something that makes me take a moment to pause and reflect on my heart motives. Am I loving my devotion to Jesus or Jesus Himself?

When we lay down our own plans, and actually submit them to God, He can then refine and purify our desires, motives, and methods of fulfilling our destinies, and in exchange give us a life *truly* abundant.

When Jesus asked me to lay down my dream of being a leader in the company I loved for many years, at first I was sorrowful, much like the rich young ruler. Jesus didn't chase after him though, and Jesus did not have to chase after me. I may have been disappointed for a moment, but because I trust who Jesus is and I trust that God is good at being God; I knew He had something better in store for me. Quite honestly, it took a lot of faith, and a lot of *building* my faith, to walk the next few years without a real end goal, or 'purpose' in sight. I had no idea what was next. He called me to be home. He said I was done. I had no idea what to expect.

I trusted Him. I trusted Who He has been to me in the past, Who He was to me at that moment, and Who I believed He would be to me in the future. He had never failed me yet. I knew I wanted His best for me, and if He was telling me I wasn't there yet, I was willing to seek **Him** to find it. I knew I needed to be led by His Holy Spirit. The Bible says that there is a way that seems right to a man but the end of it is death. (Proverbs 14:12) If we allow the Holy Spirit to lead us in every season we can be *sure* that we are on the right path.

I had to wait. His Word for me in that season was to *wait on Him*. I had to remind myself, *"Those who wait on the Lord shall renew their strength…"* (Isaiah 40:31) Are you in a waiting season? Waiting to hear a solid word from Jesus for direction in your life? Waiting for His promise to come to pass? In those times it is essential that we rest, rejoice, and allow Him to rejuvenate us in the waiting room. It is that indefinite space where we must learn to just be. This can be so difficult.

For me, it took *years* to learn how to *just be*. Just be His. Just be content. Just be willing. Just be obedient. He had to weed so much out of my heart and motives. He had to teach me how to see Him move in the daily small steps of obedience. When He taught me, then He showed me how glorious those small steps are because I began to see His finger prints all over my life and the lives of those around me! It is truly a blessing to be a blessing to others. *That* is true fulfillment! Walking in the footsteps of Jesus and being sure of it!

I learned how to find contentment in the calling of where I was in that specific season. We all go through different seasons that are meant to shape us to be more like Christ. Some are called to be caretakers of the home and/ or children; others are called into the corporate world or to be entrepreneurial. Some people are called into ministry; others are called in a little bit of each of these areas. Whatever the season we find ourselves in, if God has called us there, we must be content where we are. This is why it is so vital to continue to press in to have a constant, vibrant relationship with The Lord. If we know and trust Him, we will have confidence in our season and be sure of His leading.

As I trusted, and waited in the darkness, slowly The Lord helped lead me to the mountain peak to watch the sunrise over the valley I had journeyed through for years. The light slowly illuminated the dark places in my life and I began to gain understanding for the seasons He had brought me through. I also began to trust Him on a much deeper level. We all go through times of mountaintops, and times of desert valleys; it is how we grow and become more like Jesus. The valleys and deserts are there to refine us, purify us and to get 'Egypt' out of our hearts. They are meant to shape us to be more like Him. The valleys are designed to help us draw closer to Him.

Each time we go through a valley we should rejoice because if we are following Him; we have gained a deeper level of intimacy with The Lord. It may take some time to really reflect and see it; but it is through persevering in the valley that we gain the glow of Jesus.

After The Lord humbled me and told me I was done trying to live my own dream, I wasn't instantly put into the roll He is calling me to now. He had to take me through the refining process in the valley. There was much work to be done, and there still is. I began to realize my life was less about me, and needed to be *all* about Him. If we lose our lives, we gain it (Matthew 10:39). We cannot cling tightly to our own lives if we are to be Disciples of Christ. God had to refine my stubborn heart that wanted to listen to every other guru, expert, and successful person out there *before* listening to Him. He had to strip me of my pride, my accomplishments, and the way I thought about them and idolized them.

Is there anything wrong with accomplishing big things? Absolutely ***not***! Where God has placed you, ***shine*** like a city on a hill! Nevertheless, be sure it is *God* who puts you there to shine, and not your own self. Moreover, if there is an attitude or heart shift needed, allow Him to make that shift in you.
Trust me; if you ask Him, He will show you.

A question I was terrified to ask at this time was, "What if He takes away everything I have gained?" It was a real fear. When we work so hard for something unknowingly apart from Him, or make our own plans hoping for His blessing, as I once did; it can be a terrifying thing to actually let Him have a say in our journey.

I heard Lysa Terkeurst speak at a conference and she explained my heart condition at this time perfectly, 'God here's
my plans, (my dreams, my goals,) now could you just bless it? Don't mess with it- just bless it!'

By doing that we keep God at an arm's length away. I know I was afraid to ask God what He wanted me to do after I found out my dreams were not His idea for my life. However, I learned that we cannot fear! God is *not* a God of destruction of His people, but *RE*-construction. God is *not* a God of chaos, but of order. God is *not* a God who causes misery, but Who makes beauty from ashes!

Our destiny is to be so intimate with The Lord that our walk is His walk. And His Way is narrow.

As Christians, we tend to think of 'the way' as being to simply believe in Jesus, but the Bible says that *'even the demons believe and they shudder'. (James 2:19)* I even think we examine this passage of James and see how it's easy to think that if we believe and *do good works* in the name of Jesus that we are walking the narrow way. However, my thoughts are brought to the passage that says that in the day of Jesus' return the people say, *'Lord, Lord, we cast out demons in your name, we healed the sick in your name… and the Lord says, 'depart from me I never knew you.' (Matthew 7:22-23)*

That is pretty incredible, and these are the words of *Jesus* Himself. Believers, who did works of ministry and deliverance for The Lord, but don't **know** Him… This is why intimacy with The Living God is so incredibly ingrained on my heart. We **must** *know* Him, or all is for nothing.

In the parable of the 10 virgins in Matthew 25: 5 were wise, and 5 were foolish. They all knew *who* Jesus was, and were expecting to go in to the marriage feast, but only the 5 wise who had their lamps filled with oil were prepared to go in. The others were underprepared; they had oil but not enough- and they were not allowed to enter the marriage feast.

I believe the oil is symbolic of The Holy Spirit. Having a relationship with The Lord in our lives and being filled with His Spirit is *essential* to our walk. Otherwise we will be caught off guard, believing we were just fine being overall good people and having the salvation prayer as our backup plan. However, He gives this parable because He desires that we would be prepared to be in intimate fellowship with Him and be ready for something as sacred as a marriage feast. His love for us is so great, which is why he warns us to be careful and watchful. He desires for us to be deeply connected with Him.

When Christ was raised from The dead by the power of The Holy Spirit, He imparted The Holy Spirit to dwell in us. It is so imperative that we do not ignore this gift but continuously seek to "fill our lamps" with His presence so we can operate in His Spirit.

The Scripture says:

> *There is a <u>way</u> that seems right, but the end is death (Proverbs 14:12)*

The true Way is Jesus. *"I am The Way…" (John 14:6)*. Looking at the walk of Jesus through the gospels, *His way* was watching what The Father was doing and doing it. He was constantly led by The Holy Spirit. That is true intimacy. He *knew* His Father, and said we ought to know Him in the same manner. However, in our western culture it is so easy to be clouded with distractions and our own thoughts and other voices, it can be difficult to hear Him clearly and see what He is doing without being extremely intentional.

God is *alive*, *active*, and *moving* in the earth! Let's wake up to what He is doing and take notice of Him! I know I desire to be a part of what *God* is doing; not what I *think* He is doing; not busy with what I think I *should* be doing because it's a 'good' thing.

I have experienced days where I am in prayer and God places a scripture, a song, or a topic on my heart; only to attend a conference, meet a friend for coffee, listen to the radio or go to church and hear the exact same thing from the heart of the Pastor / speaker, friend, or that song is playing on the radio! When the Holy Spirit moves and leads us we get encouraged by incredible confirmations like this!

The question becomes, is it The Holy Spirit truly leading me? If we cannot answer with a definite **YES**, then let us dig deeper into the heart of God; this is His desire!

We are not meant to be stagnant; we are designed for constant pursuit. If we are not moving forward, then we are moving backward. There is no staying comfortable in one spot. It is a slow fade into who we used to be before Jesus entered in to the picture if we aren't intentionally growing and challenging our faith. Apostle Paul said he runs the race, because even as an apostle doing the will of The Lord, he had not obtained the prize yet. This statement in Philippians 3:12-14 was toward the end of Paul's life. This catches me off guard because after he was saved from being such a radical and wicked man he literally devoted the entire rest of his life to sharing the gospel, the good news of Jesus Christ everywhere he went and was thrown in prison, beaten until near death multiple times. And yet he knows the true prize is not obtainable here. He's reaching *beyond* into eternity. The prize is *Christ*... it is knowing God.

> *"Therefore, let us strip off every weight that slows us down, especially the sin that so easily trips us up. And let us run with endurance the race that God has set before us. We do this by keeping our eyes on Jesus, the champion who initiates and perfects our faith…" (Hebrews 12:1-2)*

We are to yearn for Him *'like a deer pants after the water' (Psalm 42:1).* These things I am asking God and myself, 'what does this look like in my life?' We will never be perfect, but we are supposed to try to be holy as He is holy in our conduct. *(1 Peter 1:16)*

Our goal should be to become as close with Him as possible which makes us more like Him. Living in the world we live in, we cannot excuse ourselves to be *like* the world, there is to be a difference. *"Come out from among them and be separate, says the Lord." (2 Corinthians 6:17)*

We are to be in the world *but not of it*, a *counterculture*, not a subculture. Going against the grain in love.

What is different between *us* and the spiritual guru who believes in being one with the universe? What is the difference between the joy and peace *we* carry and someone's positive vibes? Does the world see the difference? Or is it enough if we simply give the credit to Jesus for our good life?

We must truly reflect. How does Jesus actually *shine* through our gifts and our actions? Are we really making Him known? Are we really living free in His name? Are we really living out the testimony that He gave us? He brought me out of darkness! I once was lost but now I'm found! If I am not living to make this evident, then I am letting others down! I'm hiding my lamp under a bush! And subsequently I am robbing Jesus of His rightful glory!

I know I want to be constantly bettering myself for Him. Not for anyone else's approval, but for Him and to help others know they can experience His love in a profound way like I have. By focusing on Him we know that we will be challenged by Jesus; sharpened, focused, and we will grow. We should never want to stop growing. Let us dig in to gain a deeper level of trust with Him as we follow Him to fulfill our call and purposes in our lives.

The Mark of Moses...

At the time of Moses' death, The Lord takes him to the top of a mountain to show him that his mission is complete- the Israelites are delivered and about to enter into the Promised Land.
It was time for Moses to move on to his next mission. I look at this section of scripture and think there was probably some exchange here that was private, just between these two. 'Ok Moses, behold the fruit of your labor. Are you ready to enter eternity with me? I have an even better place than this Promised Land that I am giving your people. But know your people have reached their destination I assigned you to help them reach. You have fulfilled your mission'... and then The Lord sent the spirit of Moses to the heavens and buried his earthly body there.
The Lord blesses Moses with another personal encounter on a mountaintop overlooking all of the hard work he had done, paying off. He was able to be in the presence of the Lord, just as he desired, until the moment of his last breath.

Let's Pray

Lord, I lift up those reading these words right now and bless their journey. I pray that you would challenge us to look inward. Let us truly pause, reflect, and ask You, The Maker of us all, "Oh, Lord... what *is* your plan for me?" I pray as we ask the tough questions, if what we are doing is truly the *best* You have for us, that we will release everything to You and allow You to hold it in the palm of Your ever capable hands. Help us to boldly march forward in the confidence of *fulfilling* our calling and destinies.

Please Lord, let us continuously examine our hearts, and let us continually seek Your face, Your approval, Your wisdom, Your favor, Your will. If there is anything in our lives that we are chasing after that is competing with *You*- rid us of it now, in Jesus' name. Crush everything that has raised itself up as an idol, or anything we blindly have placed on that pedestal ourselves. Lord, be the true center of our drive and passion.

Lord, have your way in our businesses, ministries, careers, home life, friendships, relationships, and even our hobbies. Lord help us to continue to trust you on a deeper level every season of our lives. Build our faith, stir up the gifts within us, and deepen our devotion to You.

Lord, in every area of our lives that we are called to, whether it is a friend, a coworker, a sister, a brother, a daughter, a son, a mother, a father, a husband, a wife, a grandfather, a grandmother, a business owner, a neighbor, a servant, a leader, a minister... let us fulfill Your call to be all You have called us to be in these various roles.

Straighten our paths, and renew our hearts and minds today, help us to refocus, because you are not the destroyer of our lives, but the re-constructor. Take our lives into your hands and help correct anything we have allowed that isn't in perfect alignment with Your plan. Humble and soften our hearts to accept Your will and plan for our lives, and help us walk obediently, day by day to fulfill your plan for us and become who You've called us to be. In Jesus' name. Amen.

Reflect

In what ways can you do small acts of obedience for God?

What has He asked of you recently?

If you aren't sure what He has said recently, can you remember the last *powerful* impression He placed upon your heart?

Have you fulfilled that one thing? Have you gone back on it, or ignored it completely?

I urge you to pray and ask God what the next step of obedience is for you to accomplish and ask if there is anything you missed. Be still for a bit and reflect.

What comes to mind?

IGNITE

"Igniting others is a mark of intimacy with Me"

*When we **walk** in purpose, we begin to **fulfill** our destinies, and others see that the freedom of purpose in Christ can be theirs, and their hearts **ignite**!*

Once we are ignited for Christ, everyone around us begins to catch on fire; burning passionately to let the world know the love and life that awaits them.

Throughout my journey with Jesus, like most people I have had my ups and downs, my highs and lows. But I recall at one point feeling particularly mediocre.

I was attending church, praying sometimes, reading sometimes.

But I was busy.

I was so busy I just wasn't experiencing God like I had before. Once I finally *made* the time to sit down and talk to Jesus about this, I realized I was a lot less satisfied than I thought. "Jesus, I am not hearing from you like I was. I'm not able to journal, I can hardly find time to read Your Word, and I just feel blah!" This is something like how my conversation began with Him. It wasn't more than a couple days later that I had a divine intervention.

Three of my closest God girlfriends and I were scheduled to get together and celebrate a birthday. We got together at a restaurant and ordered every desert on the menu and began chatting away. It wasn't too long into our evening when one of us began opening up our hearts about her current dissatisfied state in *her* relationship with Jesus; much like my situation I just described to you.

Once one dear heart opened another, and another. We were all bearing our souls and before you know it we were praying over each other in the middle of that restaurant.

That's nothing abnormal for us. We are connected by Jesus; and even when we gather for an everyday purpose, it's all about Him.

Nothing seemed to physically snap, or emotionally change immediately. But you better believe that something happened in the spiritual realm that night.

As I look back I envision my heart being something like a smoldering coal; hot but not flaming. But once the prayers were released that night that smoky coal of a soul burst into a flame and once that flame was kindled, Jesus began to fan it hotter into a blaze.

It was the vulnerability of a few ordinary girls that led to walking out a small step of obedient prayer that unleashed an ignited group of souls. I didn't know it then, but each of us had a powerful shift in our hearts that night. Like the Scripture says, as iron sharpens iron, so a friend sharpens another. *(prov 27:17)*

That night, the fiery love of The Father was in each of us, and as we prayed each of our hearts were contagiously ignited. The Bible says the world will recognize us by our love. If we are Christians not known by love, then we are clanging symbols, and a loud gong, and are of no use to God. Basically, we are just a bunch of noise, in an already noisy, chaotic world. *(1 Corinthians 13:1-3)*

If all we do is complain about others and their sin, or the way they are wrong, we are no better than they are. It is much better to live a pure life and focus on Jesus than to focus on the way others are living contrary to God's Word. True freedom is found in taking our eyes off how others are living the *wrong way* and placing our gaze on <u>The Way</u>, Himself. We need to lead by example through enjoying a pure life all for Jesus. Yes, we are to be accountable to one another; if someone sins against you or you against another, we are to resolve it. *(Matthew 18:15)*

According to Luke 17 1-4 we must also walk in continual forgiveness and not allow our hearts to be bound up in offense. If we allow offense to hide in our hearts they become hard and then we are not truly putting on Christ. *(Romans 13:14)* We need to be careful of this one because Jesus was very clear that if we do not forgive others our Heavenly Father cannot forgive us. Unforgiveness is something God will not allow. It isn't a sin that is simply covered by the blood of Jesus. It is something that must be *constantly* repented of. Because the very blood of Christ was shed for <u>our</u> forgiveness, it is to trample on His blood if we don't extend the same forgiveness. *(Read Matthew 18: 21-35, Mark 11:25, Ephesians 4:26-27 &31-32, Hebrews 12:15 & Colossians 3:13).*

In Roman's 1 & 2 Paul addresses being an upright follower of Christ in a fallen culture and how to handle it well. We are not to condemn but to remember that *we were once darkness* as they are, but now we are light. If we are truly going to help others we need to remember what great a debt Christ paid for us, how much forgiveness we have received and help others come out of that darkness too.

James says, *"My brothers (*he is speaking to believers*), if anyone among you strays from the Truth and falls into error and another person brings him back to God, let the (latter) one be sure that whoever turns a sinner from his evil course will save (that one's) soul from death and will cover a multitude of sins. (James 5:19-20)*

Therefore, we know that as followers of Christ, *we* can stray. We can get a little off course, apparently even *severely* off course since James says whoever turns that sinner from his evil course will save his soul from death and cover a multitude of sins. We can fall into error, but James does not say we should condemn or slander that person, he suggests we are to help turn our brothers and sisters away from that evil.

When I think of how Christ graciously turned me away from my sinful ways before I knew Him, He did not send others around to condemn me; they sure did speak truth, but it was all saturated in the love of God. I think of my own walk and how I have strayed away at times; it was the pure lives of those around me and the conviction of the Holy Spirit that drew me to repentance. The process of going from glory to glory is different for everyone, but this just proves my point even further. If we have a deep, abiding relationship with Jesus, we will see others through His eyes. We will ignite passionately for Him, and that fire will be a torch for others to see in the darkness that surrounds them; and they will find their way back to the path of Christ.

In Galatians Paul says to the believers, *"Brothers, if any person is overtaken in misconduct or sin of any sort, you who are spiritual (who are responsive to and controlled by the Spirit) should set him right and restore and reinstate him, without any sense of superiority and with all gentleness, keeping an attentive eye on yourself, lest you should be tempted also. (Galatians 6:1)*

So we need to be prompted by The Holy Spirit to help our brothers and sisters stay the course, and at the same time check our own hearts to be sure we are walking humbly and uprightly.

"Love covers a multitude of sins" (1 Peter 4:8).

My mind instantly goes to "a whole bunch". However, the word multitude here in the Greek is <u>*not*</u> "Ochlos" which means: "a crowd", or "much", or "great". This word signifies a great many people (like the crowds of people described in the instance of the loaves and fishes).

The word Peter actually uses here is: <u>*Plethos*</u>, which means "a fullness". So what this means is: love covers the fullness of sin at its depth and core. Walking in love is how Christ walked. He brought conviction, and encouraged people to repent; all the while, walking in love. When we walk in love it helps turns people from their selfish and sinful ways, and helps us to bear one another's burdens.

When we are ignited for Christ, it is because of the incredible love that we have stumbled upon. Our eyes being opened for the first time, and the flame of passion being fanned by the Love that God so passionately and unwaveringly holds for us. We are the apple of His eye. We are His masterpiece. His fingerprint. His workmanship. We are wonderfully made, and artfully created. We are made in *His* image.

He seeks us out through the storms of life, all the while calling out to us, the ones whom He so dearly loves. He is jealous for you, my friend. So passionately jealous for your time, your heart, your gaze to be upon Him and for your soul to be ablaze for Him.

Building intimacy with Christ is a journey that *never* ends. Because He is inexhaustible, we continue to know Him in so many different ways in our own hearts and minds. When we recognize the purity of His love for us, there is no way we can possibly deny it. When we experience His love in a revelatory way, we can never be the same.

I've begun to realize: it isn't enough for us to talk about how our walk as Christians is "not a religion, it's a relationship". We must now ask ourselves, "What *is* a true relationship with Christ?" "What does it look like?"

Let's read the following as an example of how we relate with Christ, Himself.

A relationship by definition is: A connection, association, or involvement; a connection between persons by blood or marriage, an emotional or other connection between people. Yes, it is an affiliation, an alliance, a bond, etc. But some other defining attributes of relationships are also: communication, dependency, an exchange, a kinship, and nearness. These words imply a deeper intimacy than someone you are simply acquainted with. We aren't meant to simply be introduced to Jesus and be affiliated with Him like we've joined a club or organization. We communicate with Him, we depend on Him, we exchange words and emotion with Him, and we experience a nearness to Him.

When we look at how the Bible defines our relationship with Jesus it has the ability to take on multiple forms of depth.

We are called:

Sheep: Psalm 23:1 Matthew 9:36
Servants: John 15:15/ Philippians 1:1
Friends: John 15:15
Brothers: Hebrews 2:11
Children: 2 Corinthians 6:18
Bride: Revelation 19:7

Our relationship and level of intimacy builds simultaneously as the flames in our hearts ignite. But we don't simply inherit these titles. These different ways we relate to Him are layered in the process of our journey. We need to intentionally seek them out.

> *"Our relationship and level of intimacy builds simultaneously as the flames in our hearts ignite."*

Let's talk about what truly ideal relationships should look like. Servants are cared for, and expected to respect and serve the master. Friends connect on a deeper level, and share thoughts, feelings and journeys together. Brothers share blood, share parents, and they love one another. Children depend on their Father for their needs, regardless of earning that care. They are loved, cared for, taught right from wrong, guided, disciplined, corrected, empowered, and given responsibility. A bride is cared for in an even more passionate way, being physically and emotionally cared for, listened to, and sacrificially loved. The Groom so loves the bride that He would give His life for her to protect her.

These are the aspects of relationship The Lord desires to have with us. I remember first exploring this reality in my thoughts, and struggled with some aspects of these relationships. What if you're not emotional? What if you don't want to submit as a servant? What if you had a horrible child-parent relationship? What if you were abused? What if you had a marriage that ended badly? What if you were abandoned? What if the only one(s) that seemed to care for you had died? What if the way you have related to others so far has been tragic, or has even left you jaded?

Then, in our own strength it could be more difficult to trust God. Nevertheless, by God's perfect love and matchless grace He can show us how to trust Him. He can show us that He is indeed a good Father, a good Master, a good friend, and The True Lover of our souls. Truly, He redeems those aspects of relationship in our lives and heals our wounds. This is why He died for us: to redeem!

Important Scripture truths for us to think upon:
God is not a man that He can lie. (Numbers 23:19)
God makes all things to work together for your good (Romans 8:28))
God will not give you a stone when asking for bread (Luke 11:11-13)
When we trust in Him with all our heart and stop depending on our own understanding He will direct our paths (Proverbs 3:5)
He is our provider, He is our healer, He is our refuge and very present help in times of trouble. (Psalm 46:1)
He is all sufficient for us. (Genesis 17:1)

In addition to having life circumstances paint our perception of relationship with Jesus and Who He is; a difficult thing in the culture we live in today, is that many of us equate seeking Jesus with attending church or being a part of a church group. We can even go to church with misguided motives; and the problematic issue is that it is difficult to detect if we are.

We may attend church to be social. We may desire to fulfill the need to belong. We may want something that is more exciting, or entertaining. We may want to hear a certain type of message that motivates us to live a better life and make us feel good inside. We may go out of guilt or shame and try to get right with God over and over again because we continue to live in a perpetual state of struggling with the same sin. When we struggle in that way it is because we haven't actually done away with the old man and put on the new man yet. (Can you tell I've been here before?) It is exhausting seeking God this way. Is it sinful for us to desire to find community, excitement or freedom when we go to church? *Absolutely not*. However, again we are dealing with motives.

It is so accessible to pick and choose here in America where we would like to go, what we would like to hear. We want instant gratification. If we don't get what we are looking for we can go somewhere else to try and get the feelings we are looking for. In their song "O God forgive us" by For King and Country they sing "we want instant hope and drive through peace", I have seen this in my own life and if we aren't cautious it can become about what makes *us* happy and less about what makes *Jesus* happy.

In the first century church they didn't have these choices to make. They just *were* the Body of Christ. They met together in homes, broke bread with one another, sought God and struggled through grave persecution.

It is also far too easy for us to hear a good speaker, preacher, or encourager, and think of how profound *their* revelation is of Jesus. Sadly, that is what it ends up staying: **their** revelation. To us it is just intriguing knowledge. It is not personal or revelatory. It stays a lofty theological idea. It hasn't sunk into our soul to help it become a transformational truth. Oftentimes we can have the tendency to backslide in our behaviors, thoughts or feelings because we have no true personal revelation knowledge of *Who* Jesus Christ *really* is! I pray for this revelation knowledge to continue as we walk with Jesus through our days on this earth. As we read His Word, I desire that we continue to gain fresh revelation *every time*.

I had heard message after message of walking upright before The Lord, rededicating our lives or walking in the miraculous, but until I sought God *myself* and let Him ignite me it was just words and wishes.

I read an article by Ryan Shaw that struck my heart entitled: *"Embracing Our Calling as 'expendables' for Christ"*. He explains that during war, men of unusual courage were called upon for difficult assignments, and often these men did not return from war. They were called "expendables." His writing portrays how our calling for Christ mirrors this: to lay down our lives. The disciples laid their lives down for the cause of Christ because Christ laid His life down for us; we ought to be willing to lay our lives down in the same manner. A statement that caught my eye was this: *"...When moral compromise, lukewarm love for Christ, biblical illiteracy, prayerlessness, self-absorption, idolatry, greed and pride mark multitudes of believers today, we need a massive rearranging of our priorities."*

I believe that in general, our convenient western culture breeds these things in the larger Church, and the *mark* that he speaks of is reminiscent of what Christ describes as spewing out of His mouth when He comes back for His Church. *(Revelation 3:16)*

Jesus is looking for the *Mark of Moses*; the mark of intimacy. The ones who will pay the price like the ones who have gone before us. The ones who will climb the mountain *just* to be in His presence when everyone else is too complacent, distracted, or afraid. He is looking for the *wise* virgins, the ones not only knowing He is coming, but the ones who are eagerly and *preparedly* awaiting His return! He is coming back for His closest of friends, His most faithful bride. I desire to be ready for Him. I desire that you, my friend, are ready as well. Truly, we should all, as Paul says, *'take heed lest we fall' (1 Corinthians 10:12)*.

Becoming best friends with The Holy Spirit should become our aim. He is the promised gift- the One Christ died to send us. He is the empowerment. The One who draws deep into The Lord. He is the connection between us, The Son, and The Father. He longs to speak to us, to be our Comforter and our Guide. He longs to take us from glory to glory *(2 Corinthians 3:18)*.

I fear that oftentimes He goes unnoticed, ignored, and pushed aside. It can be a lot of work to hear His voice; a lot of time spent pursuing and seeking. And sometimes, let's be honest; it's easier to just talk about Jesus and do some good in His name, than to actually *walk* the *walk* that Jesus asked of us. Do we understand the taking up of our own cross means this Jesus walk will take some effort and leg work? *(Matthew 16:24)*

This walk ain't no joke! This is a path that might be straight and narrow- but it's full of mountains and deep valleys! And thank The Lord we have been equipped to handle it by His grace but we also have to *activate* the tools He's given us to make the trek!

I am not talking about working to *earn salvation*, we cannot do that. I'm talking about the desire of *The Living God* Who wants to know you and for you to know Him on a deeper level than you can fathom!

He desires to be your Shepherd and walk you through the hills and valleys along the path of your life. The Holy Spirit is such an incredible gift, because He equips us with knowledge, understanding, wisdom, discernment and helps us to navigate our lives. He is the manifestation of the presence of God; the One Who ignites our hearts.

I was at a nightly prayer service one evening and became somewhat overwhelmed with things going on in our world and culture. However, during worship a song welled up within me. Not a song that I heard on the radio or in a church service, but something from inside of my spirit. I continued to repeat, 'Nothing but You…. Because of You…'

It didn't make sense to me at first but sometimes that's how we know it's The Lord speaking to us. We think, "Where in the world did that come from?"

As I repeated this to The Lord I was thinking about all the things we can be against; how we can take a stand against things we think are wrong, or even take a stand *for* things we think are right. However, all I could hear in my soul was that *none* of it is *worth my worry;* what *truly* matters is focusing on The Lord. It can be so easy to let the cares of this world consume us and tear us to shreds on the inside.

Nevertheless, let us come to focus on *nothing but Him because of Who He is*. Instead of allowing the cares of this *world* to consume us, we must let Him and His wisdom, His love, and His sovereignty consume us!

No *cause*, no *rights*, no *theology*. Just simply Him, because of *Who He is*; because of what He has done; because He is *The* Way, *The* Truth, and *The* Life. He is all we will ever need. Intimacy with Him is the answer to all of our struggles. Through being close to Him, we hear Him, we see what He is doing, and we can experience Him more fully and respond to the world around us with His heart. When we go through difficult times, we can have comfort, hope and a peace that does not make sense.

The reason I will choose to focus on Him - just Him - is because of Who He is and all He has done for me. I have seen His hand of deliverance on my life; experienced His immeasurable forgiveness and have basked in His sweet presence. He is my all in all and I grow more in love with Him daily.

After Moses completed his mission, Joshua was left to carry on the flame and passion and example of Moses. Joshua was anointed by Moses to carry his mantle, and finish leading the people of Israel to the Promised Land.

My deep desire is that you too, would gain an even deeper passion for The Lord than you ever thought imaginable. That your heart and spirit would be ablaze for loving the One who passionately loves you more than you can understand. And friends, *we have not arrived!* Don't give up or lay back when you think you've got it all figured out and have this great Jesus relationship- *push deeper*!

Through each of us gaining a deep, intimate relationship with The Lord, and continuing to go deeper; we will set the world on fire, full of fierce love. And we will truly be a city on a hill that cannot be hidden.

The Mark of Moses...

In Exodus 33:15 Moses tells The Lord he doesn't want to go to the Promised Land unless God's presence goes with them. "For your presence among us sets your people and me apart from all other people on the earth" ...

In other words, Your presence <u>*MARKS*</u> your people. And Moses understood the value of this.

In essence, Moses is saying he would rather <u>*stay*</u> in the wilderness and be in the presence of God than in the Promised Land without him.

<u>Moses wanted the PRESENCE of God, more than, the PROMISES of God.</u>

It's this kind of fiery passion for our Lord that can ignite our hearts- "Lord, if You're not in it- I don't want it! Only where your presence goes!" Let us develop and deepen this kind of relationship with Him!

Let's Pray

Father in Heaven; let us lay aside all things that so easily trip us up. Let us daily seek your face, walk full of faith, and walk in steps of obedience. Let us desire to make You smile. Let us fulfill your daily desires for our lives; and through Your Holy Spirit led obedience, let the hot embers in our souls be fanned into flame, set ablaze for you, and catch the world on fire.

We need You more than ever. Have Your way, Oh Lord. Draw us into Yourself. Help us to go from glory to glory and experience a deeper level of intimacy with You. Help us to understand every facet of relationship we are designed to have with You. Awaken the areas of our souls that are sleeping. Reignite a fiery passion within us. Let us open Your Word to gain a deeper understanding and revelation of You. We want to know You more, Oh Lord. Fan the flame in our souls, Lord. Fan the flame ablaze. Ignite us In Jesus' Name.

Reflect:

Have you been feeling like the flame in your heart has become embers? What do you think has caused the flame to dim? What can you do to help reignite the fire in your heart again?

Have you found yourself to be more judgmental or critical and less helpful and encouraging to those in a struggling state? Let's pray for God to help us to have His eyes of compassion.

How can you allow the love of God to move through you to the people around you?

How do you think loving those around you in a deeper way (through Christ's eyes) could help them draw closer to God?

How can you take a step back and allow The Holy Spirit to blow on the flame in your heart?

Echo

"To Echo My work is a mark of intimacy with Me"

*When we begin to **fulfill** our daily purposes with Jesus, the spark of passion **ignites**, causing the **echo** of true identity in Christ to ripple.*

When I think of an echo, I think of sending something out, and having it continue to make waves. To me, an echo means that everything you do impacts *more* than yourself. His words travel to our hearts and echo out to the world around us. What we do, how we respond to people, how we respond to God, how we pray, how we listen, and how we love; all of these things touch the entire world around us, one small ripple at a time. These ripples affect negatively or positively, and we should be aware that whether negative or positive; it is a choice.

Deuteronomy 30:19
"Today I have given you the choice between life and death, between blessing and curses…"

Spend any amount of time with a small child and you will soon see an echo in action; words or mannerisms. Anyone who has ever met my son (especially when he was a baby) has told me that he looks identical to my husband. "He looks nothing like you Crystal; he's a spitting image of his father." Sounds harsh, but it was true. Especially if they were in the same room, there was just no denying they were kin. The important thing is: I know who labored for 16 hours. This girl. That boy is *mine*!

The thing was, even at his young age of around 3; not only did he *look* just like my husband but he *acted* like him too! I have an entire scrapbook page in his baby book dedicated to this notion. They would sit the same way, sleep the same way, smile the same way; sometimes it was scary. It was especially scary when I'd hear something negative come from his small mouth and realize, "Ohp! There I am..." (I'm from Minnesota, we say "Ohp"). It's in those moments where I check myself and realize that I am making an impact.

Every day the choices we make in word and deed will affect the people around us. In my case, it will especially affect my son's life. And in turn it will affect those that God places around *him*!

This is our legacy in action; to echo Christ to the family entrusted to us and all who God has allowed in our lives.

As influential as those moments of learning are for me; it is equally significant when I hear my sweet boy utter a bold prayer with authority and reverence for God. *That's* the kind of influence I want to have on my son. The kind of ripple effect I'm supposed to have on the world around me. Sometimes that boy's faith can be so bold and pure it makes my heart quake. As he's growing, I'm seeing him pray with bold faith like his mama and worship with abandon like his daddy. These are the echoes that matter most in life. How does the nature of God displayed *in* us, influence the world *around* us?

When we truly love God and others the way that He loves them, we begin to fulfill our destiny. When we begin to fulfill our destiny, we help ignite others on fiery passion for The Lord, and that fire continues to spread for generations to come. An echo. A ripple effect.

Metaphorically, there are paralleling aspects when we look at the sun and moon relationship and our relationship with The Living God.

Just like the moon, destined to reflect the brightness and fire of the sun, we are destined to reflect the glory and life of our King in Heaven. The reflective rock of the moon absorbs the glory of the sun and does its best to illuminate the darkness. It is beautiful, it gives off light, but no matter what, it can never *outshine* the passionate fire of the sun. The sun is red hot - so marvelous it cannot be touched - so incredibly powerful that its warmth and rays give life sustaining energy to the entire earth.

The moon goes through seasons. Sometimes you can only see it partially shine. But it is when the elliptic longitude of the sun and moon differ at 180 degrees from each other that you see the moon at its fullest and brightest.

Psalm 91:1 says, "He who dwells in the secret place of the Most High shall remain stable and fixed under the shadow of the Almighty {Whose power no foe can withstand}

It's almost as if after being 'close' to the sun for its appointed season, under the shadow of its greatness- absorbing all of its strength, light, and brilliance; it can then be 'sent off' to gloriously display the reflection of the sun.

The sun is constant, and always beaming brightly to help bring life and encouragement for the moon to keep shining on. Like the moon; we were destined to reflect The Son.

Having a close relationship with The Lord; being stable under the shadow of The Almighty is so vital. If we dig into Psalm 91:1 further, the word "secret place" is: Satar, or Samek. The Samek is a little rounded vessel with a flat roof or cover. Poetically in Hebrew this would represent the heart of God. This means that *those who dwell in the heart of God* will find shelter. As we press in to the heart of God and gain intimacy with Him; He covers us and brings us stability, protection, confidence and restoration.

I believe it is also essential to have a wise and godly encourager and to be discipled in the faith, if we are to have a victorious walk. It is key for us to find someone who emulates or reflects Christ and His love and is willing to listen, teach, guide and point us to Scripture. Once I had someone come into my life that was older and wiser, who was there for me, who loved me for me, who watched my walk carefully, who led me to scripture, who prayed for me like a warrior, and who loved me fiercely; I began to grow and flourish like I never had before. A supernatural breakthrough began that propelled me into growth and toward my destiny.

The disciples went out in pairs and always held each other accountable. When the disciples spoke, it echoed the teachings and the heart of Jesus. Jesus was their teacher; their first example. After that, Jesus commanded them to go and make disciples in all nations; to echo what He had begun. And today we are still echoing this because of the waves made by The Original.

When we echo the true nature of Christ people are drawn in to meet The Original. It isn't *really* by our elaborate programs or events that people get saved. We don't have to try to 'lure' people in to the faith. What draws them is *The Spirit of God* as we truly echo His nature and love. Isn't it freeing to know that it's God *through* us that draws people to Himself?! I don't have to *strive* and *struggle* to come up with the most creative, intricate plan to bring people into the Kingdom. My job is to be obedient to God; He will do the rest!

> "When we echo the true nature of Christ people are drawn in to meet The Original."

I have felt the sweet and gentle shoulder tap from The Lord and He tells me, "Crystal, you're good.... But you're not *that* good." … He's keeping me in check! Making sure I don't try to take what is not mine. I cannot take His glory- because it's truly His power and Spirit that draws mankind to Himself. But I also should not take a burden of guilt. When things don't go how I think they should, I do not have to bear that burden. If I know I am being obedient, I don't have to worry or fear if the numbers aren't where I think they should be, or if the prayers aren't being answered how I *want* them to be. I can trust that **_He_** is the one who is God and He is good. It is our job to know Him so we can echo Him.

Moses lived most of his life being completely faithful to God. He was faithful to deliver the 10 commandments, faithful to seek God, and he desired the presence of God over the promises of God. However, there was one point when Moses sinned by openly disobeying God. He sinned in his anger, and that sin in the desert bred disrespect for God among the other Israelites. After that, God did not allow him to enter the Promised Land.

That may seem like a harsh punishment; however the actions of Moses led to a *negative* **_echo_** against God.

We need to be careful that what we are sending out with our actions, our integrity and our words are glorifying to God, or there will be consequences. Whether or not God would withhold a blessing from us is not the thing we should be concerned with.

What we need to focus on is asking ourselves this question: Is what I am sending out going to breed disrespect or disobedience to God? I may not be responsible for other people's actions, but I have an *influence* and I need to take full responsibility for that. Is the way I'm reflecting God to others drawing them closer to God's heart and encouraging them to truly press in to Him more?

I've been convicted before about discussing a hurt or offense that someone caused me. But this is also known as gossip. The Lord is very clear that we are not to be a part of gossip. In Romans 1:29 it is labeled wickedness. In 2 Cor. 12 19-21 Paul mentions how it is a sin that grieves. Proverbs 26:20 says, *"Fire goes out without wood, and quarrels disappear when gossip stops."*

I'm thankful for a good friend in college who took this kind of integrity to heart in her own walk with Jesus. If I ever began to discuss an offense she would graciously cut me off and tell me she didn't need to hear it to guard her own heart. I learned really quickly to discern in my own heart when I was offended and to try and quickly catch if I began to gossip. It is a very hurtful thing to be caught up in gossip. Whether you are the subject of it or it is coming out of your mouth. Of course gossip is only one aspect that can negatively impact others. Truly for us to display Jesus and His heart to the world we must honor others and honor Christ. That is why Jesus told the disciples that the greatest commandments are to Love The Lord our God with everything we have and love our neighbors as ourselves. When we do this, and honor those as God would and honor those as we would desire to be honored, then we are echoing Jesus well.

Now, Moses also had an incredibly positive echo, as I've stated before: Moses was known as the most humble man on the earth. He was also known as a great prophet. None were like him that knew God face-to-face in the way that he did. Moses' heart was aimed at obedience to The Lord, and although his one mistake wasn't taken lightly, it didn't corrupt his echo forever.

When we look at the end of King David's life as he is passing the throne over to his son, Solomon; he gives a command: *"Keep the charge of the Lord your God, walk in His ways, keep His statutes, His commandments, His precepts, and His testimonies, as it is written in the Law of Moses, that you may do wisely and prosper in all that you do and wherever you turn…" (1 Kings 2:3)*. Even King David respects and recognizes the echo that Moses made for generations.

Another question to ask ourselves is this*: Am I reflecting the love of The Father, or am I reflecting the ways of the world?*

I think it is vital as we continue to walk in intimacy with The Lord to be mindful of our impact on the world around us. We should be prepared to walk as a leader of God knowing that we have a higher responsibility as we begin to send things out into the world.

There was an instance where God really stretched my family and me with a next-door neighbor we had. We lived in a townhome complex and had a Bible study one night per week. One evening after Bible study was over, everyone was leaving and we were saying our long Minnesota goodbyes. My son became full of energy and started running around like a puppy across the floor on his hands and knees. About 10 minutes later this neighbor came loudly banging on the door just as people were exiting my home. She pointed at my son irritably as he stood at the top of the stairs as if to discipline him. I could see she was full of anger, so I went down to meet her. As I opened the door she began to yell and scream loudly and complain about how loud we were being. I tried to stay calm and tell her that everyone was leaving now and we would not be disturbing her any longer. The calmer I was the angrier she became. It escalated more and more until finally I had to ask her to leave my property. Let's just say it didn't end on a great note. I knew we really weren't being that disturbing. Listening to worship, praying and talking was not something new, and my son's burst of energy was short-lived.

I'll tell you what was really going on in that moment. Satan was angry. That night girls were crying and set free from emotional bondage and the presence of God was in our home powerfully. Satan will do that. He will send people your way to try and take away from the anointing God is giving you. But we need to recognize when the enemy gets angry and not take offense. We have to let it roll like water off a duck's back. We have to try and remember that we do not war against flesh and blood. (Ephesians 6:12)

After the girls left I won't lie, my emotions were a bit heightened, and my adrenaline was pumping. But I knew what we needed to do in that moment. Jesus said, *"bless those who curse you and pray for those who mistreat you"*. (Luke 6:28) (Matthew 5:44)

If your enemies are hungry give them food to eat. If they are thirsty, give them water to drink. You will heap burning coals of shame on their heads, and the Lord will reward you. Proverbs 25:21-22 (also found in Romans 12:20)

Love your neighbor as yourself. (Mark 12:31)

So, we prayed for her. We felt led to write her a small note of apology, and give her a token of our love. We left it in her door and were sure to let her know that she is loved by God. After that her communication with us became actually pleasant for the first time. We never had another issue with her again and she began to smile and wave at us. What a difference the way of Jesus will make!

I definitely could have chosen to act out in my flesh. Part of me wanted to. But thank The Lord His presence hadn't left my home. He guided us that night to do what Christ would have done. Show that woman how powerful the love of God *really* is.

As I influence the people around me: my family, my friends, the people with whom I come in contact; I want to be sure that I am always pointing everything back to Jesus. I want to *echo* His heart for those that I am impacting. If there is ever any glory to be had, it must go to The Lord. If there is ever anything I do well, it is because *He* has first empowered me, and given me the gifts that I have, and I always want to be sure to point directly back to Him. If there is anything I do well to encourage someone else, I want those people I've impacted to know: without a doubt, it is The Holy Spirit Who is empowering me. It is God Who is utilizing me as a vessel to bring The love and encouragement of God to someone He wants to inspire that very moment.

We have learned to carry on this Echo through the great examples of heroes in the faith who have gone before us. Even looking at the life of Joshua as he learned from Moses himself! Joshua would wait outside of the tent of meeting as Moses and The

Lord spoke face-to-face. He watched, waited and learned. He knew that Moses was being led by God and that what they had was wonderful enough to wait and glean from. And once Moses passed, Joshua continued to echo the same reverence for The Lord that Moses did because He understood what effort it took to pursue intimate fellowship with The Living God. And he knew the fruit of it.

Friends, He loves you so fiercely. He desires more than anything to have intimate fellowship with you.

You are *chosen* (Ephesians 1:4). Do we truly understand the gravity of this statement? He has *chosen* you for *His* pleasure. He is *pleased* with the plans that He has for *you*. It's not just a big lump sum of people He wants to follow Him like blind robots. He has a *very* specific and strategic calling that He has chosen specifically for *you*, that *only* you can fulfill. You will impact the people around you in a way that *only* you can. You will do certain creative things that *only* you can do. We need to *live* like we are, in fact, chosen.

Do you truly *know* that you have been adopted into the family of God? Do you know that He chose you from the foundations of the world; since the beginning of time? Do you know that you are the apple of His eye? Do you know that you specifically have a calling and a destiny that only you can fulfill in this beautiful tapestry of life?

I pray that God would give everyone reading, this revelatory knowledge; a supernatural understanding of the truth of who you are in Him.

You are made in His image, and He has a good plan to prosper you. I hope you know in the core of your being that when you step into His plan, it *will* affect not only you, but the people around you for The Kingdom of God. He has positioned you, just as He positioned Esther to help save the nation of Israel. You have been called for such a time as this. However, just like Esther, you have a choice to say yes, or to say no. Her uncle Mordecai encouraged Esther, *'Who knows if you've been called for such a time as this? But if you don't go, God will surely raise someone else to deliver Israel.'* (Esther 4:14)

You have been called. Yes, you. I'm talking to you. The one sitting there reading thinking this doesn't apply to you for some reason. You have some excuse? You think you're too old? Too young? You've messed up too many times? You don't have the resources? You don't know where to start? You don't have a passion? Your life is ordinary? Your life is too difficult or complicated?

So it was with Moses, and Abraham, David, and Esther, and with Jonah…. In the beginning of their spectacular journeys they were just as ordinary as we are. Shepherds, servants, plain people… plain people who believed God.

Moses was living the ordinary life of a shepherd. Abraham was too old to have a child. David was too young to beat Goliath. Esther was ordinary, yet was called into the palace for a unique opportunity. Jonah had no compassion to help sinners, and he ran away from God's calling. David messed up and then repented. And yet God still used all of them; despite their human inadequacies.

Jesus said, *"My grace is sufficient for you, for my strength is made perfect in weakness" 2 Corinthians 12:9*

This grace Jesus spoke about is an *empowering* grace. It is the supernatural ability to do what we cannot do in the natural, which is why He says His strength is made perfect in our weakness. His strength shines by means of His grace when we are weak.

We have no excuse. The Bible is full of the beautiful plans of God manifesting in many ordinary people's lives… who all had an excuse. But by their surrender to God they have left ignited passionate marks on the past generations that are still burning brightly today and being passed on continuously. You have a purpose, you have a calling, you have been chosen, you have an impact, and you have a legacy to leave. A beautiful echo of God to release on the world around you.

Shine brightly my friends.

The Mark of Moses

Not only is Moses' life a depiction of how we should humbly walk our faith out and relate with The Living God. But I also view Moses' journey as a type of foreshadowing or symbolic parallel to the life of Jesus. Although, Moses is simply human and cannot compare to the Lord Jesus Christ; I find it quite amazing how God chose this one son to be set apart. This one son was raised in royalty, went to the wilderness, received a fire encounter with The Lord, and (eventually) answered the call to deliver God's people.

Like Jesus Who came from Heaven (in royalty). Was born in a manger; a humble way to make an entrance as The King (a lot like how Moses was the most humble in the world). Not only was Jesus sent to the earth (like the wilderness) but He was also led into the wilderness before He received the fire of the Holy Spirit. After His testing He began His ministry- answering the call to deliver God's people.

How incredible to see a foreshadowing of The Lord, Yeshua; Jesus Christ. To see that God had a redemptive plan all along, and has a redemptive heart for us. He has laid out an example. He has shared His secret with us. Drawing near to Him is the key.

Let's Pray

Lord I pray that you would, right now, speak to our hearts. Holy Spirit, would you bring us a revelation knowledge and understanding of our worth in the eyes of The Lord. Would you help ignite the dream in our hearts?

Show us the calling we have been chosen for, show us how to walk intimately with You in a new way that would bring us even deeper with You.

Help us to be ready to influence generations to come, and make us ready to leave an eternal impact. Help us to desire to _echo_ _You_ in our lives, at whatever capacity you are leading us to.

Lord help us to identify with someone in the Bible that we can relate to. Lord help us to find a godly teacher or someone to mentor us so we can be sharpened and equipped and encouraged to go forth into the call that You have placed on our lives.

Help us to truly love you, truly love others, and walk forward into the calling that you have for us. Lord let us echo you in the best way we can. In the mighty name of Yeshua.

Reflect

What call have you felt on your life? Are you acting on it?

In what ways do you feel you emulate Christ best?

What ways do you feel you are living, speaking, thinking, or acting that *contradict* the way Christ lived? And what ways that are *congruent* with the way Christ lived?

Do you feel you have missed your opportunity? If so, how can you envision God redeeming your story and restoring any mistakes you feel you've made? (If He did it with Moses, Jonah, Ruth, Paul, etc… He can do it for you too!)

What dreams have you had that you've placed on the shelf? Do you feel God leading you to trust him for this on a deeper level?

Who is Moses?

In general, I think most people would recognize Moses as a baby who was fished out of a river, raised in the palace; later, met God at a burning bush, parted the Red Sea, received The 10 Commandments and led God's people to the promised land after 40 years of wandering in the desert.

Let's look into the first 5 books of the Torah, or the Old Testament… the books Moses actually wrote. When I did this for myself, God revealed His unique relationship with Moses to me in a very special way. There is a lot that happened in the 40-year journey. So after reading, studying and praying I tried to keep it to the highlights of how The Lord and Moses developed an intimate relationship.

While you may have heard the story of Moses, or may have studied it intensely, I am praying that God would give you a fresh reminder, or even a new perspective of this ordinary man who had an extraordinary relationship with The Living God. This, I believe, is how The Lord desires His relationship to be with us as well.

Exodus

SCRIPTURE SAYS...
We start off in Egypt. After Joseph had passed away, a new Pharaoh had risen up and as God's people (Israelites) had multiplied, Pharaoh became fearful they would rise up against him and overthrow their land, so he ordered them to become slaves. However, the people continued to

multiply, so Pharaoh ordered all the Israelite boys to be killed. (Ex. 1:22) Despite Pharaoh's orders, the mother of Moses kept the baby hidden until he was 3 months old, built him a waterproof basinet and set him in the river where the Pharaoh's daughter would bathe. She found the baby, crying, had pity on him, and hired the baby's own mother to nurse and care for him until he was old enough to come to the palace and grow up as her child. She named him Moses because she drew him out of the water. (Ex. 2:10)

Let's talk…

Ok, can we just take a minute and look at this? God has a divine plan for each of us. God knew all along what this child would grow to do, and had a purpose in keeping him alive. God protected Moses and used Moses' mother and the daughter of Pharaoh to raise him up under protection, and even in the palace as a Hebrew.

So far, Moses' story shows us that God does indeed have a plan for us, not just to use us to do mighty things, and not just to bless us, but He is a strategic God. He is also a loving God who will go to great lengths to see His will in our lives is accomplished.

Scripture says…

Moses grew up in the palace, and one day when he was a grown man went out among the Hebrew slaves. When he saw one of them being beaten, he was so moved to protect one of his own (Hebrew) relatives, he killed the man who was abusing the slave, and then exiled himself and ran out of fear. (EX. 2:15)

Let's talk…

So… Moses had murdered in vengeance? Yes, and yet God didn't intervene at this point. It's almost as if God's hand was *still* guiding Moses. In fact I believe it was. However, don't let this taint your view of the man of God Moses was. I think sometimes we forget that God has never changed. He was The Redeemer and Forgiver even before Jesus came to display it in the flesh, and He is still the same today. He looks at the motives of the heart, and we are about to see more of Moses' heart here now.

Scripture says…

Moses made his way to Midian. Along his journey, he found 7 daughters of a priest who were in need of protection, and he stepped in and helped them. The father was so grateful for the justice and kindness Moses displayed, he allowed Moses to marry one of his daughters. They married, had a son, and lived in Midian for a while, until one day God intervened.

The Lord had heard the cry of His people in slavery and was about to recruit Moses for one of the most dangerous, top secret missions out of anyone yet recorded in the Bible.

One day, while ordinary Moses was tending to his father-in-law's sheep, he went to the back side of the desert, at the bottom of the mountain of God (Mount Horeb or Sinai). There an Angel of The Lord appeared in a blazing fire out of the middle of a bush, but the fire wasn't consuming or burning the bush to ash. Moses said aloud that He was going to stop and look at this great sight, because the bush wasn't burnt. The Bible says that when The Lord saw that he stopped to look, then God called out from the middle of the bush, and called Moses' name. Moses answered. (Ex 3: 1-4)

Let's talk...
So let's just look at this. God is watching His people, hearing their cry. He is watching Moses, and while in the midst of something as ordinary as caring for the flock of sheep, God gets Moses alone, and gives him his first recruitment test. Is Moses up to the challenge? We might think of the challenge as confined to delivering God's people, but the biggest life call of Moses begins here: will Moses *listen* and *respond* to God's voice? Next, we have the very first interaction between Moses and The Living God.

Scripture says...
Moses replies to The Lord, "Here am I." Then God says, "Don't come any closer, take off your sandals, for you are standing on holy ground, I am the God of your father, the God of Abraham, Isaac and Jacob." When Moses heard this, he covered his face because he was afraid to look at God." (Ex. 3:5-6 NLT)

Let's talk...
The Lord Himself is audibly speaking to Moses. Not only that, but we see Moses' response. His response is full of awe, wonder, and reverence for The Lord. He immediately responds by covering his face because he is afraid to even look at The Lord, because of His holiness.

Scripture says...
The Lord proceeds to speak about His desire to free His people from their slavery, and even says Himself that He has **come down** just to deliver His people. He has a land prepared for them according to His will; a land flowing with milk and honey.

God tells Moses He has chosen him to go to Pharaoh to free His people. But Moses protests to God, ***"who am I?"*** And yet, God replies, "I will be with you."

Moses protests again, **"what am I supposed to say?"** God replies, "I AM WHO I AM. Tell them I AM has sent me to you. YAHWEH has sent me to you, this is my eternal name." The Lord also told Moses to tell them that He has SEEN how they have been treated and that He has promised to rescue them from their oppression and even explains what will happen as He goes to Pharaoh. Yet, Moses protests again, ***"What if they don't believe me?"*** So The Lord, being patient with him, asks what he has in his hand. Moses explains it's his shepherd staff. The Lord commands him to throw it to the ground, and it immediately turns to a snake. After The Lord's command to reach out and grab its tail, it turned back into a staff. "Perform this sign," The Lord tells him, that then they (the Egyptians) will believe him. The Lord then tells him to place his hand inside his cloak, when he removes it, it is covered in a skin disease, after he places it back in his cloak as The Lord instructs, and removes it again it is perfectly healed. The Lord said if the first sign does not convince them the second one will. Finally, The Lord says if they still didn't believe him after the second sign to take water from the Nile River and pour it onto the dry ground, when he did, the water would turn to blood on the ground. (EX 3:13-15, 4:1-9 NLT)

"Oh Lord, I'm not very good with words." The Lord asks Moses, "Who makes a person's mouth?" In response, He tells him to go, and that He will tell Him what to say and be with him. (Ex. 4:11)

Yet Moses protests AGAIN, ***"please send anyone else!"*** at this point The Lord became angry with Moses and suggests Aaron, his Hebrew brother go with him and that He will be with both of them. Moses will relay God's voice to Aaron, Aaron will be the mouth piece, and Moses will use the Staff to perform the miracles God had just shown him. (Ex. 4:13-17)

Let's talk...
Let's just look at this first interaction. It begins as a holy moment, but soon Moses' futile human reasoning begins to set in.

Who am I? Don't we oftentimes think we are just not adequate for God's great call in our lives? Moses was just an ordinary man, as we are all just ordinary. But that is the beauty of when God calls us to Himself. He makes us something beautiful. We need to learn from Moses and his list of excuses or self exclusion to the call of God. Because God clearly says that He will be with us; eliminating our inadequacy because He is more than adequate. ***What am I supposed to say?*** After God assures us He will walk with us step by step, we can still be like Moses, thinking 'ok, maybe you'll be with me, but how do I even begin? What am I supposed to say? How do I even start this crazy journey you're asking me to go on?' Again, we feel inadequate and even unfit for the call. We also get scared off by the 'what ifs'. And yet God assures us of WHO HE IS. This is an important piece.

God doesn't say, "Moses! You tell them God has empowered you, and sent you to deliver them and has made you great so they should listen to you!" He tells Moses who HE is. Sometimes we need to be reminded that HE IS GOD and I am not. That He IS THE GREAT I AM. There is nothing too hard for Him. We need to be reminded that not only will He be with us, but also to ask ourselves, DO WE EVEN KNOW WHO HE IS that is promising to go with us? What better promise *is* there? Not only does The Lord assure Moses who He is, but He gives him a message for his special people, that He sees their oppression. He shows such care and concern for His people. How beautiful; He is God, He sees the wrong in our lives, and He has promised to rescue us.

"What if they don't believe me?" The Lord's response is the miraculous: signs and wonders that He begins to display through Moses' obedience. There are many times throughout scripture that due to our human doubting and reasoning God shows just a glimpse of His power through signs and wonders, and this is one of those incredible times. Not to mention, this is Moses' third protest and The Lord isn't angry or frustrated, but he patiently answers his concerns. I believe it wasn't only for the Egyptians to have a sign, but also for Moses to help his unbelief. God is revealing His power to Moses and even *through* him in this very intimate and exclusive moment at the bottom of the mountain. Another thing I love about this moment is The Lord is most likely expecting another excuse from Moses, so he reveals 3 miraculous signs in a row, stating if they don't believe because of this, then show them this, if not those two then show them this. Sometimes aren't we just like this? 'Oh Lord, I don't know… if you're REALLY speaking to me, I need a sign, I need another sign, how about a third sign?' Yet, He is patient like a loving Father.

"Oh Lord, I'm not very good with words." Enough with the questions, here come the excuses about WHY he feels disqualified. What shortcomings do you have that make you feel like God won't use you? I think there are many things we allow to get in our way because we are worried about what man thinks, or how people perceive us. Yet, God reminds Moses again WHO He is; that HE is the One who made Moses' mouth. We need to be careful we do not disrespect God's creation (us). He made you perfectly 'flawed' the way you are, and He will use you in spite of those things, because His strength is made perfect in our weakness (2 Corinthians 12:9)

"Please send anyone else!" 'Anyone but me Lord!' 'You've got the *wrong* person.' Have you ever felt this way? 'I think you dialed the wrong number Lord, you've got 7 billion of us now, and maybe you got me confused with someone else?' 'I think you lit up the wrong bush, Lord.' As silly as this sounds, we think this way because we are human. Just like Moses, we are ordinary human beings, and we should always remember that. Do you know why we should *always* remember that? Because it is very important as we go further in the story of Moses that we remember that Moses is *just as human as the rest of us*. He exhibits the same fears, the same shortcomings. He has even sinned, just like the rest of us. Even after all of the miracles and wonders that God does through Moses, using Moses to deliver His people, and all of the other amazing and incredible feats that God did *through* Moses, Moses is still an ordinary human.

What makes him extraordinary is *only* the level of intimacy he developed through obedience with The Creator. The Lord's response to Moses's final protest in essence is Him saying, 'Fine! You can bring a friend!' So his brother Aaron was allowed to go with him. As a pair they helped lead the people of Israel from Egypt.

So, to fast forward a little, The Lord sends a message to Pharaoh through Moses. However, God hardens Pharaoh's heart in the end to show His glory the strongest and to execute judgment in Egypt. He wants His glory to be made known (kind of like how He didn't want Moses to have an excuse about the Egyptians believing him, so He gave Moses 3 different physical signs to display), so The Lord knew that the Israelites would be sharing these miraculous signs and wonders for all time, generation, after generation. He couldn't just bring them straight to the Promised Land; He needed to *show* His might and power so no one could ever doubt that it was *Him* and His hand alone that delivered His people. No one else could take credit.

But even through this, Moses shows his humanity. In Exodus chapter 5:22 Moses says "Why did you send me?" and even questions The Lord, noting that Pharaoh has been even more brutal and God has still not rescued them.

Don't we get impatient with the process sometimes? 'Lord, I thought you were doing this great thing, but it's looking worse now that I've *begun* my journey.'

SCRIPTURE SAYS...

Yet, God persists because He sees all things and knows all things. He reassures Moses in his doubting. The Lord explains to Moses again what He will do, and then we see something that not only catches my eye, but catches my heart. In verse 2 of chapter 6 The Lord tells Moses "I appeared to Abraham, Isaac, and Jacob as El-Shaddai (God Almighty), **but I did not reveal my name, YAHWEH, to them.**

LET'S TALK...

WHAT?! Did you catch that? This is powerful. Yahweh is The Lord's most holy Name.

Yes, The Lord *did* reveal Himself in a special way to Abraham, Isaac, and Jacob; as El Shaddai (God Almighty), but the first person He ever told His *redemptive name* to is Moses. This is a level of intimacy that can easily be glossed over when we don't understand the significance. The God of the universe reveals different aspects of Himself throughout scripture so we can get to know Him more. But what is amazing to me is how He uses His journey *with* Moses to reveal so many different aspects of Himself to him, and to us. Revealing His name Yahweh to Moses, is likened to a best friend revealing their given name that nobody knows.

SCRIPTURE SAYS...

In Chapter 6 The Lord reveals His redemptive Name to Moses, and encourages Moses to tell the people of Israel that The Lord sees them and He will in fact, deliver them. However, we see that they refused to listen to Moses because they had become too discouraged by the brutality of their slavery.

LET'S TALK...

Have you become too discouraged to listen to God's message to you? Have you been under the brutality of the slavery of the world for too long? Have you become discouraged because you feel that The Lord has not kept His promise to you? In other words, when living in bondage under the things that weigh us down in the world for so long, without fully allowing Jesus to lift the burden, we can become jaded.

I'm here to tell you, please listen to this redemptive story, and please receive its message of hope into your heart. God is not a man that He can lie

(Numbers 23:19). The Lord has a plan for you, He may have even revealed it to you, or given you a glimpse, but you have yet to see it pass. Do NOT give up.

Do not grow weary in acting nobly and doing right, for at the proper time you will reap a harvest if you do not give up. (Gal 6:9)

Sometimes we think God has forgotten us or is even taking too long to answer our prayers, but that is not so. *"For God is not unjust. He will not forget how hard you have worked… and how you have shown your love to Him." (Hebrews 6:10)*

"The Lord isn't really being slow about His promise, as some people think. No, He is being patient for your sake." (2 Peter 3:9)

God needs to refine us. He needs to help us get to the point where He can utilize us in the area He has prepared for us. As you wait, I pray you would find rest in waiting patiently, give Him your heart and your aspirations and let Him do a deep work in you. As we become pliable clay in His masterful hands, He is able to mold us and shape us into the beautiful creation He has destined for us to be. Let Him have His way.

After we see how discouraged the Israelites are, we also see the discouragement of Moses. Again he points to his clumsy speaking, and even though God has already answered this complaint, He commands them (Moses and Aaron) to go free His people.

Are you like Moses? In the middle of your calling, but feeling like it's not working, like something is off? I encourage you to keep going, and keep pursuing God and His vision for your life. If you are off kilter, allow God to straighten your path. Moses had a view of trying to free God's people with his *own* words, in his *own* strength. But The Lord was trying to get him to realize that it was only by *HIS* mighty strength that this would be accomplished; God would in fact use Moses to set His people free, which is why He told him simply, to go.

SCRIPTURE SAYS…

We begin to see the plagues that were unleashed according to the hardened and disobedient heart of Pharaoh. The plagues were as follows: blood in the waters, frogs, gnats, flies, livestock killed, boils, hail storm, locusts, darkness (so thick you could feel it - and yet not touching the area of the Israelites dwelling), and finally the death of the first born sons of Egypt.

The Lord then led them from Egypt, and instead of taking them on a straight path right to the Promised Land, The Lord led them in a pillar of cloud by day, and a pillar of fire by night, so they could travel at all times. The Lord led them to the Red Sea where they thought they would perish, but God commanded Moses to raise His staff. The seas parted so there was a giant wall of water on either side of them, and dry ground to walk on through the middle of the sea. (Exodus 15)

Let's talk...

First of all, why did The Lord lead them the long way away from Egypt? Was He cruel? Was He trying to kill them as they complained? Of course not. In fact, it was *a severe mercy*. The Lord needed to lead them through the wilderness to prepare them and strengthen them so they would not want to turn back to Egypt. He knew the hearts of the people, just as He knows our hearts today. He knew if He led them straight to the promises they would immediately forget all about Him, and He wanted to show them His supernatural hand and reveal parts of Himself they did not yet know. Can we just reflect on this a moment? The God of the universe wanted to reveal Himself to His people. He wanted to dwell with them, get to know them. So, he took them on a super long camping trip! I've heard people say before, if you want to know the real heart of a person, go camping in the wilderness for a week. The point is, when we're under pressure, our ugly starts to come to the surface.

The wilderness is training ground to help us grow, so that we will NOT desire to go 'back to Egypt' or back to the world; back to the way we used to be. Sometimes the desert is tough, and the journey is longer than we would like, but look around you! The Lord is showing Himself to be strong all around! He desires that you seek *Him* instead of the promised land.

Reading about Moses raising his staff and The Lord parting the seas is where we really begin to see Moses recognize that God is the One Who is delivering the people. All he needs to do is walk obediently.

Scripture says...

At the Red Sea, The Lord parts the waters for about 600,000 Israelites to pass through, once they are all through, The Lord commands Moses to raise his staff again, and releases the walls of water on the entire Egyptian army, delivering the Israelites from them all, just as He said He would.

As The Lord leads them through the wilderness He provides manna and quail from Heaven for them to eat, and provides water from a rock for them to drink. He performs miracles and signs from Heaven to display His glory to the Israelites.

Unfortunately, after all The Lord has done, the Israelites continue to complain, disobey and harbor idols in their lives. They constantly wish to go back to slavery and live under oppression being 'fat' with whatever they want (with food, possessions, etc.). I believe this deeply hurts The Lord's heart. Each time the Israelite's disobeyed God and wouldn't listen, and would continue to complain, The Lord would say to Moses "How long will these people refuse to obey my commands and instructions? (Ex 16:28)

In Chapter 19 we see God ready to meet with His people. Remember, up until this point He has been in the form of a pillar of cloud and a pillar of fire leading the people away from Egypt.
I've heard teacher John Bevere describe this moment like Moses was facilitating a meeting for the first time; a grand introduction. Moses climbs the mountain to appear before God, and God gave His instruction to Moses, the Israelites said they will do what The Lord says, so Moses climbs back up the mountain to give the people's response to The Lord. The Lord says He will come down in a thick cloud so the people can hear Him when He speaks to Moses, so they will always trust him. Moses was then told to go prepare the people for God's arrival. When The Lord comes down the mountain, thunder roared, and lighting flashed, a dense cloud came down the mountain, and there was a long, loud blast from a ram's horn. The people trembled. (Can you imagine this sight?!) All of Mount Sinai was covered with smoke because The Lord had descended on the top of the mountain in the form of fire, and the whole mountain shook violently. Then the Lord called Moses to meet Him at the top, so Moses climbed the mountain. This is when God began to give Moses the 10 commandments. After the incredible sight the people of Israel witnessed, they were terrified to the point they told Moses that he should be the only one to talk to God, they were sure they would die. So in a sense, they rejected personal communication with God. They preferred to have a messenger to relay His words.

The people of Israel weren't even allowed to climb the mountain where God was residing. In Exodus 24 we see The Lord says, *"Only Moses is allowed to come near to The Lord. The others must not come near, and none of the other people are allowed to climb the mountain with him." (24:2)*

It was shortly after this that The Lord descended over the mountain in a cloud and Moses climbed higher to meet with God personally, and *"he remained with God 40 days and 40 nights. When the Lord finished speaking with*

Moses on Mount Sinai, He gave him the two stone tablets inscribed with the terms of the covenant, written by the finger of God." Ex 31:18

Disappointingly, during the 40 days and nights that Moses was gone; the Israelites became impatient and demanded that Aaron give them a god to lead them. Aaron was seemingly easily persuaded and had them give him their gold, which he melted down and made into the shape of a calf. The Israelites worshipped it in place of The Lord their God, and exclaimed that "these are the gods who brought us out of the land of Egypt!" The next morning Aaron helped them build an altar to their new god and they made sacrifices and a feast, and 'they indulged in pagan revelry.' Ex. 32:6

The Lord told Moses, "Quick! Go down the mountain! Your people whom you brought from the land of Egypt have corrupted themselves. How quickly they have turned away from the way I commanded them to live! I have seen how stubborn and rebellious these people are. Now leave me alone so my fierce anger can blaze against them, and I will make you, Moses into a great nation." Ex. 32: 7-10

Let's talk...
Moses, being the friend of God that he was, interceded for the people and tried to pacify the anger of The Lord his God. He actually helped change God's mind.

God has emotion. We can provoke Him to jealousy and even anger when we refuse and rebel and continue to be stubborn in our own ways. He desires us to desire Him but He won't force us. He is the same yesterday, today, and forever.

Scripture says...
When Moses climbed down the mountain and saw everyone celebrating he burned with anger. So much so that he threw the stone tablets to the ground, smashing them at the foot of the mountain. His fierce passion for The Lord was so strong he couldn't stand to see the people hurting The Lord in such a way. As an intercessor, I believe Moses felt The Lord's pain, and experienced a portion of The Lord's anger.

After he disposed of the idol they had been worshipping, he then desired to make things right and went up the mountain again to try and beg God to forgive them. When he spoke with The Lord, I think it's a beautiful picture of his intercessor heart. "...if you will only forgive their sin—but if not, erase my name from the record you have written!" (Ex 32:32) The Lord replies, "No, I will erase the name of everyone who has sinned against me.

Now go, lead the people to the place I told you about. My angel will lead the way before you."

Let's talk...
At this point in the story, (Exodus 33) I see two main things that strike me as extraordinary. The first thing is that Moses had a 'Tent of Meeting', where he would meet with The Lord to bring the requests of the people to Him, and intercede. Whenever Moses would go to the Tent of Meeting, all of the people would stand and watch him enter. As Moses would enter the tent, the pillar of cloud would come down and hover at its entrance while the Lord would speak to Moses "face to face, as one speaks to a friend" (33:11)

How incredible is this? I think this is fascinating to ponder. That, in these times, God couldn't speak face to face with anyone, except for one man. The friendship they had is incredible, intimate, and one of a kind. It shows the desire of God's heart to commune with His people, and it is due to the obedience in Moses' heart, and his desire to please The Lord.

Despite Moses' shortcomings in the beginning of his journey, and his questioning God, Moses builds a relationship of trust with The Living God, and develops a unique relationship where they were like friends who would meet and speak face to face.

If you think this is incredible, just wait. The next part is my favorite! It gives an added glimpse into the friendship that they had.

Scripture says...
Moses says, "You have told me that You know me by name and you look favorably on me. Let me know your ways so I may understand you more fully and continue to enjoy your favor."

The Lord responds, "I will personally go with you, Moses, and I will give you rest - everything will be fine for you."

Then Moses said, "If you *don't* personally go with us, don't make us leave this place. For your presence among us sets your people and me apart from all other people on the earth." (Ex. 33:15)

Let's talk...
Hold on a minute!!! Let's go back to verse 3: The Lord said to Moses, "Get going to the land I swore to give. But I will not travel among you, for you

are a stubborn and rebellious people. If I did, I would surely destroy you along the way."

When we fast forward to verse 15: "If you don't personally go with us, don't make us leave this place."

Moses is making a statement here that I think is absolutely essential to *our* walk of faith with God. Moses is in essence saying he would rather stay in the wilderness and be in the presence of God than in the Promised Land without Him.

As John Bevere breaks it down in his book, Good or God:
Moses wanted the **PRESENCE** of God, *more than*, the **PROMISES** of God.

Wow. The man who spent day after day in the presence of God- face to face- knew a secret. I think we need to get in on this secret.
To dwell with God in His presence is sweeter, richer, more satisfying, more gratifying, more powerful, and more absolutely quenching than *any* promise He offers. Although His promises are great- I need to ask myself, am I thirsting for the right things? Am I thirsting for His presence more than what He can offer me? If not, I need to know Him more! I need to dig deeper, press in harder and realize that there is something missing if this is not my aim and goal.

Do we desire the sweet presence of God more than we desire all of the blessings that certainly are ours to have? It is a difficult place to be when we live in the Western culture and everything is at our fingertips.

But this is where I want to be. This is where my heart is being led. I want to sit in God's presence, to dwell in it, to meet with Him, to hear from Him, to act on behalf of His love, and His passion for His people. I want that more than any promise I could have of abundance, or prosperity, or healing, or anything! I just want Him. And I think His true desire is for each of us to find this secret place of dwelling face to face with Him.

Scripture says...
The exchange only becomes more incredible between The Lord and Moses after this. Moses says to The Lord, "Show me your glorious presence." The Lord says He will put Moses in the crevice of a rock on the mountain and will cover him with His hand until He has passed by, and will remove His hand so he can see His back briefly only as He passes by, but His face could not be directly seen because Moses would surely die. (Ex 33:18-23)

In Exodus 34 Moses spends more time with The Lord rewriting the stone tablets. When he came down the mountain His face was glowing from speaking with The Lord! It scared the people so Moses ended up placing a veil over his face until he would speak with The Lord again.

In Numbers 12 we see a glimpse of how The Lord feels about Moses. I'm reminded of when Moses fumed with anger because of the people worshipping the golden calf, and how he defended The Lord. In this section of Numbers we see some people had become jealous of Moses' calling and felt like Moses had gotten special treatment. In verse 3 it notes that Moses was very humble. In fact it says that Moses was **MORE HUMBLE THAN ANY OTHER PERSON ON EARTH.**

The Lord hears the complaints of the people and rebukes them by saying this (paraphrased), "Now listen… I would reveal myself in visions. I would speak in dreams… but not with my servant Moses. Of all my house, *he is the one I trust*. I speak to him face to face, clearly, and not in riddles! He sees the Lord as he is…"

Let's talk
Wow! The Lord is defending His friend here. He hears complaints and has to step in and remind them that He is best friends with this man and they dare not speak about him poorly. To me, this is incredible.

The story of Moses and The Lord has a turn of events after years of wandering with the complaining Israelites through the desert. We see in Numbers chapter 20. There was no water to drink in a place of the wilderness where they stopped. So the people rebelled against Moses and Aaron. They were complaining that Moses was trying to kill them (again).

Scripture says…
Moses and Aaron went to the Tabernacle and fell face down to the ground and the glory of The Lord appeared to them. The Lord gave them instructions – now pay attention to these instructions, it is key. They were to gather the whole community of Israel (to show them a wonder and a sign of provision from The Lord), and as the people watched, to ***speak*** to the rock, and it will pour out water enough to satisfy the whole community and their livestock.

Moses took the staff, gathered the people, and said, "Listen, you rebels! Must we bring you water from this rock?" He then **struck** the rock twice with the staff and water gushed out.

But The Lord said to Moses and Aaron "Because you did not believe in, (rely on, cling to) Me to sanctify Me in the eyes of the Israelites, ***you will not lead them into the land I am giving them!*** (Numbers 20:10-12)

LET'S TALK...

What happened here was disobedience. The Lord purposefully commanded Moses to bring water from the rock by speaking to it. He wanted to give them another sign and wonder to display His holiness. However, Moses decided to strike the rock as he had in the past, and it was in direct disobedience to The Lord's command. He stole God's glory in that moment.

So we see here, this is the one time that Moses actually disobeyed a direct command of The Lord. I don't know how many times it was said of Moses in the scripture: "*And Moses did just as The Lord had commanded him*," (many, many times), however this was not one of those times.

Moses had allowed himself to be so frustrated with the continual disrespect, complaining and disobedience of the Israelites that had gone on for decades, that he allowed himself to sin and disobey God.

Another thing to note is that even though Moses protested or argued with The Lord in the beginning of his journey, He was still obedient. This time, I believe he sinned in his anger, and because of the holiness of God, Moses had a repercussion.

However, something I notice here is that Moses doesn't argue with The Lord about this. He doesn't protest, he doesn't try and excuse his behavior and say 'but Lord! The people...'

I picture in my mind that he takes the repercussion humbly because He knows The Lord is holy, he knows The Lord is just, and he does truly revere The Lord. But he made a mistake and he knows it.
Many see this mistake as a horrible tragedy. Many might even think the punishment was unjust, or unfair, or a huge disappointment after all Moses had to endure with the people of Israel. Some might even see it as a poor reflection of Moses. However, I don't see it that way, and I will share with you why that is.

As I was studying, I looked at the end of Moses' life; I saw a beautiful display of the result of walking intimately with The Lord.

SCRIPTURE SAYS...

Moses went up to Mount Nebo as The Lord had directed him to. The Lord was with him and showed him the entire land that He was about to give to the people. The Lord told Moses "This is the land I swore to give... to your descendants. I have now allowed you to see it with your own eyes, but you will not enter the land." Then... Moses died there, just as The Lord had said.
(Deuteronomy 34:1-5)

The book of Deuteronomy could've ended there. A bleak sad punishment and end to the great prophet's life. But there is more, and this next 'more' that I am about to share is what I believe The Holy Spirit has given me as a gift of a picture of intimacy, and I pray He reveals it to you as well.

Deuteronomy 34:6-7
The *Lord* buried him (direct Hebrew translation, capital YAHWEH) in a valley near Beth-peor in Moab, but to this day no one knows the exact place. Moses was 120 years old when he died, yet his eyesight was clear, and he was as strong as ever.
Deut. 34:10
There has never been another prophet in Israel like Moses, whom The Lord knew face to face.

LET'S TALK...

To me, this is powerful intimacy. It shakes my heart. YAHWEH Himself took the time and care to bury His beloved, humble prophet, and friend. They spoke every day for most of Moses' adult life, face to face, direct contact, as a friend would speak. His burial place is a secret, only The Lord knows where one of His best friends' bodies rests. Now, God knows Moses' body came from dust; that now Moses' spirit is in heavenly places. And yet The God of the universe takes the time to bury His friend's earthly body. Wow. That amazes me. It shows the love that The Father has that He can relate to us in such a way that He doesn't dismiss the things that are not eternal. He cares about the details of our lives.

I also think it's amazing to think about The Lord just bringing Moses Home. I mean, after all, Moses did desire God's presence more than The Promised Land. There is no reason for Moses to die, but he does. And if we read this with an eternal perspective, we know that God had something eternal for him to do at that point. It was time for him to move on to his next mission.

I look at this section of scripture and imagine that there was probably some exchange here that was private and just between those two. 'Ok, Moses, I showed you the land. Are you ready to come and be with Me eternally? I have an even better place than this Promised Land that I am giving to your people. But know your people have reached the destination I asked you to help them reach. You have fulfilled your mission…' and then The Lord sent the spirit of Moses to the Heavens and buried his earthly body there.

This picture that I received from God is a gift, not a horrible punishment. Yes, there was a consequence but also a severe mercy and it didn't hinder their relationship. The Lord's holiness demands justice, and The Lord could've very well just had Moses die with Aaron on Mount Hor. However, that is not what happened. Instead, The Lord blessed Moses with another personal encounter on a mountaintop overlooking all of the hard work he had done, paying off. He was able to be in the presence of The Lord, just as he desired, until the moment of his death.

The Example

Not only is Moses a depiction of how we should humbly walk our faith out and relate with The Living God. But I also view Moses' journey as a type of foreshadowing or symbolic parallel to the life of Jesus. Although, Moses is human and cannot compare to the Lord Jesus Christ, I find it quite amazing how God chose this one son to be set apart. This one son was raised in royalty, sent to the wilderness, received a fire encounter with The Lord, and (eventually) answered the call to deliver God's people. Like Jesus who came from Heaven (in royalty), was sent to the earth as a humble human (being born in a manger - humble - a lot like how Moses was the most humble in the world). Then, Jesus received the fire of The Holy Spirit when He was baptized, and began His call.

Moses had the 12 tribes of Israel; Jesus had the 12 disciples. Moses parted the Red Sea so the Israelites could cross it and enter the Promised Land; Jesus' blood is the river of living water that we must go through to enter into God's family and into redemption. Moses was a mouthpiece for The Lord; Jesus was the Lord in the flesh, and did what The Father in Heaven was doing. Moses would meet with God daily; even climb the mountain and spend 40 days and 40 nights with Him face to face. Jesus also did this often to spend time with His Father. Now, The Lord is the ultimate Deliverer, but someone had to lead the way. So Moses was called to deliver God's chosen people out of slavery; Jesus had the call to deliver God's creation from sin because He wishes that **none** would perish. Moses completed his call, and so did Jesus. Moses gave his life for the call to get God's people to their destination; The Sacrifice of Jesus was made to deliver God's people from hell. The rest was left up to the disciples. Moses went home to be with The Lord. Jesus, because of His deity and distinction, died, and on the third day rose again to take the keys of death and hell, and secure eternal life for all who would accept the sacrifice He had made and is now seated at the right hand of The Father in Heaven.

How incredible to see a foreshadowing of The Lord Yeshua, Jesus Christ. To see that God had a redemptive plan all along, and has a redemptive heart for us. He has laid out an example. He has shared His secret with us. Drawing near to Him is the key.

Seek first The Kingdom of God and His righteousness- and all these things will be added unto you.

Matthew 6:33

The Central Message

When we are *vulnerable* with The Lord it becomes easier for us to lay our *broken* pieces in His hands. When we are able to be *vulnerable* and *broken* before Him we experience a true *joy* and strength, and that *joy* empowers us to lay our lives down to Him in *surrender*. As we *surrender*, God begins to expose areas of our heart that need shifting and refining and we *repent* and see a heart change and lifestyle change. As we *repent* and begin to change we start to really **seek** God and His will more. Once we truly start to **seek** Him for more and more heart change we begin to *walk* in His way and as we *walk* with Him we begin to *fulfill* our destinies. As we are *walking* with Him and *fulfilling* our destinies our hearts catch ablaze and we will automatically *ignite* others on fire for Jesus, creating an *echo* that will ripple throughout the world and for generations to come.

ABOUT THE AUTHOR

Crystal Dill is an encourager, Author and owner of Double Take LLC. Crystal is a Makeup Artist- preparing brides for their wedding day (and helping all kinds of women discover their God-given beauty). In a similar way, Crystal's passion is to help the Bride of Christ discover her God-given beauty and potential. You can find her sharing her heart at women's events through her spoken word ministry, prayer or encouraging others with her own stories of the goodness of Jesus. When she isn't playing with makeup, writing or speaking; you can find her sharing her heart over a warm cup of coffee, or creating her Handmade Halos- a line of greeting cards. More than anything, Crystal enjoys time with Jesus, her husband James, son Lincoln and their dog Red.

Made in the USA
Columbia, SC
23 August 2018